FOUNDING SALES
—Mini—

The (Abridged) Early Stage Go-to-Market Handbook

Sales for founders (and others) in first time sales roles

PETER KAZANJY

Copyright © 2024 by Peter Kazanjy
All rights reserved.
No part of this book may be used or reproduced in any manner without written permission from the author, except in the context of reviews.
All trademarks are the property of their respective companies.

Printed and Bound in the United States by Ingram/Lightning Source

Cover Design & Book Design by Tracy Moeller
Front Cover Photograph by Jeremy Bishop/Unsplash
Back Cover Photograph by Josiah Weiss/Unsplash

ISBN: 978-1-7345051-2-2

FOUNDING SALES **Mini**
The (Abridged) Founder-Led Sales Handbook

My book, *Founding Sales*, is well known as the canonical book on founder led sales. It's designed to be a textbook-style guide for founders and other first-time sales people to learn the basics of direct selling. At 400+ pages, though, it's rather complete and detailed!

With the rise of LLMs, I figured that an abridged version, at 10-15% the size (~120 pages) might be nice as a preview to the full book. So I made just that! You can find the full, unabridged version of *Founding Sales* on *FoundingSales.com*, and the Founder Led Sales Coach chatbot at *founderledsalescoach.com*.

Contents

Introduction: How a Product Marketing & Product Management
Guy Ended Up a Sales Leader at a Public Company ... 8

Chapter 1: Mindset Changes in First Time Sales Professionals ... 10

Chapter 2: Baking Your Narrative & Product Marketing Basics ... 13

Chapter 3: Sales Materials Basics: What You Need to Sell & How to Build it ... 18

Chapter 4: Early Prospecting: Finding Your First Customers ... 29

Chapter 5: Prospect Outreach & Demo Appointment Setting ... 33

Chapter 6: Early Inbound Lead Capture & Response ... 41

Chapter 7: Pitching: Preparation, Presentation, Demos & Objections ... 44

Chapter 8: Down Funnel Selling: Negotiation, Closing & Pipeline Management ... 61

Chapter 9: Customer Success Basics: Implementation, Ongoing Success
& Renewals ... 69

Chapter 10: Early Sales Management & Scaling Concepts ... 84

Chapter 11: High-Impact Sales Hiring ... 98

Chapter 12: High-Impact Sales Onboarding & Training ... 109

Chapter 13: Where Do You Go From Here? ... 118

INTRODUCTION

How a Product Marketing & Product Management Guy Ended Up a Sales Leader at a Public Company

In 2010, our startup Unvarnished launched to massive press coverage but failed by 2011. We pivoted to TalentBin, an employee network-based referral recruiting product. As a non-technical founder, I unexpectedly became our first salesperson.

Over three years, I transitioned from a generalist to our first evangelical sales rep, then to our first account executive, and finally to a sales leader. By 2014, when Monster Worldwide acquired us, we had a team of ~20 sales and customer success staff, generating $6m/year.

This book shares my journey and learnings for founders becoming salespeople. It's specifically for B2B direct sales models, particularly in B2B SaaS startups bringing new offerings to market.

Why me? As a non-sales guy who became a sales leader, I offer a unique perspective. I had to derive many best practices, which led to strong internalization and innovation opportunities.

The book is divided into two main parts:

1. Experimentation Mode: Pre-scaling when you're just starting out.
2. Scaling Mode: Once you've figured out what works.

In the early stage, founders must do the sales themselves. Don't fall for the misconception that you can just "sprinkle some sales pros on it" and succeed. This stage requires evangelical product management and product marketing, with a tight loop between articulation, presentation, listening, and building.

You'll need to do things that "don't scale," like on-site visits for low-value deals or manual lead generation. It's about information gathering more than revenue generation.

Avoid premature professionalization. Hiring experienced sales reps too early can be a mistake, as they're not equipped for the product management and marketing aspects needed at this stage.

Don't fall for the myth of the "sales rep-less" go-to-market. Even companies like Dropbox and Twilio have sales teams. And don't think you "can't do sales"—it's a learnable skill like any other.

Remember, at the earliest stage, your success depends on an evangelical sales mindset focused on rich customer interaction and information gathering. So roll up your sleeves—this is your job now, tiger.

CHAPTER 1

Mindset Changes in First Time Sales Professionals

As a first-time sales professional, especially if you're coming from non-sales disciplines, you'll need to make some counterintuitive mindset shifts. These changes may feel uncomfortable at first, but they're crucial for sales success.

1. Embrace Plenty, Not Scarcity: In sales, time is the only scarce resource. Be ruthless about truncating unproductive conversations with marginal opportunities. There is plenty of opportunity out there, so focus on spending "good time with good opportunities."

2. Put Activity Above All Else: Sales is about activity and leverage. More calls, more demos, more proposals sent—activity in equals value out. Don't overthink or over-prepare. Just act.

3. Be Direct and Get Down to Business: In sales, you have the license to be direct. Ask about their problems, their need for solutions, and their budget. Don't be afraid to ask for the sale.

4. Build Many Shallow Relationships: You'll be interacting with dozens of new people weekly, maintaining a pipeline of concurrent conversations. Learn to quickly build rapport while juggling key deal information.

5. Assume the Sale is Inevitable: Approach conversations with the mindset that the prospect will inevitably become a customer. This frames the discussion around "when" not "if," boosts your confidence, and sets the groundwork for ongoing relationships.

6. Expect to Win, but Be Unfazed by Rejection: Project full confidence in winning each deal, but don't be discouraged when you don't. A 20-30% win rate for new, innovative solutions is solid. Learn from losses, but don't internalize them.

7. Record Everything—But Efficiently: With the high volume of interactions and the likelihood of revisiting opportunities, constant record-keeping is crucial. Use your CRM, take notes during calls, and look for ways to automate information capture.

8. Be an Expert and Fearless: Sales professionals are market facilitators, not snake oil salesmen. Become an expert in your vertical—understand the field, business processes, and competitors. This expertise will make you fearless in interactions, boosting your ability to act quickly and establish rapport. Even before achieving full expertise, adopt a fearless mindset.

9. Embrace Transparency: Get comfortable with a high level of transparency. In a well-instrumented sales organization, everything from win/loss notes to activity levels is visible. This transparency creates accountability and shared learning, driving a positive feedback loop.

10. Remember, Sales IS about Math: Don't just focus on the "right brain" activities like storytelling and rapport building. Sales involves metrics, math, and reporting. Get comfortable with CRM reports, Excel pivot tables, and analyzing data to drive decisions.

These mindset shifts are interconnected and reinforce each other. For example:

- Thorough record-keeping allows you to be direct and non-scarcity-minded, quickly identifying the best opportunities.

- Expecting to win and being unfazed by loss helps you adopt a stance of inevitability, leading to more consultative interactions and higher close rates.

- Preparing for high volumes of shallow relationships encourages efficiency in surfacing relevant business details and better record-keeping.

Remember, enterprise sales has its own "physics." Proactively identifying, embracing, and driving towards these mindset shifts will accelerate your learning curve and boost your success rate. While some shifts may come easier than others, they're all crucial for your transition from founder to sales professional.

CHAPTER 2

Baking Your Narrative & Product Marketing Basics

The first step to a repeatable, scalable sales process is building your narrative—the "story" you'll present to potential customers. This narrative will evolve, but you need a coherent rough draft to start.

For early-stage, new-technology sales, I recommend the "problem-solution-specifics" narrative framing:

1. What is the problem? Identify the business pain you're solving, as crisply as possible. For example, "Technical recruiting is hard. It's difficult to find software engineering talent with relevant skills, contact them, and manage conversations without dropping balls."

2. Who has the problem? Identify the specific person or group responsible for solving this problem. Look for those who control the budget or spend significant time addressing the issue. For instance, for a recruiting solution, target recruiters filling technical roles and recruiting managers.

3. What are the costs associated with this problem? Understand both direct costs and opportunity costs. This helps frame the ROI of your solution. For example, a CRM solution might increase revenue per rep by allowing them to handle more deals efficiently.

4. How do people currently solve this problem? Why do current solutions fail? Common answers include:

    - No solution: Your challenge is persuading prospects that it's worth solving.

    - Solution via process: Address why existing processes are inferior, often due to time costs or unreliability.

    - Existing tools: Highlight why these tools fall short.

5. What has changed that enables a new solution? Identify the technological or market shift that allows your solution to exist. For example, Salesforce leveraged ubiquitous web access to create a more accessible CRM. Understanding this change helps frame the new opportunities for your customers and supports your narrative.

6. How does the new solution work? Explain your approach, often by comparing it to existing solutions. For instance, "It's like traditional CRMs, but it uses the browser and web for access anywhere, anytime."

7. Qualitative/Quantitative Proof of a Better Solution Present why your solution is superior using the same metrics as existing solutions. For example, in recruiting, compare search result counts for specific skill profiles. Supplement with qualitative differences, but always back them with metrics where possible. Use third-party validation like customer testimonials and press coverage to support your claims.

8. Pricing Charge for your solution from the start, even if it's low. This ensures customers take you seriously and consider your value. Approach pricing iteratively, starting by giving more value than you capture. Raise prices as you gain more information about market reactions and as your product improves. Don't worry about early customers with lower pricing; grandfather them in and use it as an incentive for new customers to buy now.

Remember, your narrative should build inductively. If someone disagrees with your problem framing, you can focus on that or end the interaction, saving time and increasing efficiency.

This narrative framework will help you develop marketing collateral and guide your sales conversations. It's not set in stone—expect it to evolve as you engage with the market.

Approaches to Pricing

1. Existing Solutions Comparison: Look at competitors' pricing as a starting point. For TalentBin, we compared ourselves to LinkedIn Recruiter, offering more value at a lower price to attract customers.

2. ROI & Value Pricing: Set your price based on the value you provide. For example, HIRABL prices their recruiting agency tool based on the expected recovery of missed fees, aiming for a 10x return on investment for customers.

3. Value Alignment and Thresholding: Align pricing with value provided (e.g., more storage = higher cost). Consider pricing thresholds that allow easy entry (e.g., under corporate card limits).

Pricing to Perfection

Avoid pricing too high, as it can hurt win rates and increase churn. Start low and raise prices until you see it affecting closing conversations. Ensure the value provided aligns with the price charged.

Segmenting

Resist the urge to complicate pricing with multiple tiers early on. Focus on your ideal customer profile and keep pricing simple. You can introduce segmentation later when you better understand feature value across customer segments.

Remember, pricing is an iterative process. You'll learn more about what matters to customers over time. Don't view pricing as "done" or wait for it to be "perfect" before using it, but do have a starting point.

Putting it all Together

Your narrative doesn't need to be a formal document. Practice an elevator pitch or explain your story at a cocktail party to create a skeleton you can expand on when needed.

Here's a framework to follow, illustrated with two examples:

1. What's the problem?
2. Who has the problem? What's the cost of not solving it?
3. How is this currently solved? Why doesn't that work?
4. What has changed?
5. How does your solution work?
6. How do you know it's better?
7. What's your pricing?

The TalentBin Narrative

Technical recruiting is hard. Sourcers, recruiters, and managers struggle to find software engineers with specific skills. Not solving this problem leads to costly agency fees or delayed hiring, impacting software delivery and revenue.

Current solutions like job boards or LinkedIn fall short because few engineers actively job-seek, and many have incomplete profiles. The rise of professional activity on sites like GitHub and Stack Overflow has changed this.

TalentBin aggregates this online activity into searchable profiles with contact information. It offers 5x more results than LinkedIn Recruiter for technical searches, with 60% of profiles having personal email addresses, leading to 3x-5x better engagement rates. Available for $6,000 per user/year, it's more effective and cheaper than LinkedIn Recruiter at $8,000.

The Salesforce Narrative

B2B sales reps struggle to manage multiple conversations without dropping leads. Sales managers need to track team activity and forecast accurately. Mistakes can cost hundreds of thousands in lost revenue or missed quarters.

Current solutions like email, calendars, or outdated CRMs are inefficient and error-prone. The rise of internet connectivity has enabled always-accessible CRM. Salesforce offers a modern, browser-based CRM with the latest features and a partner ecosystem. It increases login frequency by 3x-10x, improves win rates by 20%-50%, and reduces missed forecasts by 30%-50%.

Bake That Narrative, and Then Get Ready to Make Some Collateral

Once you've formed your narrative, you're going to be taking this core story and distributing it in different formats for easy consumption by interested parties. Generally this will take the form of sales collateral for prospects, but the same narrative will get recast for other interested parties too- press, analysts, partners, and even investors and acquirers.

Now it's your turn. Answer the questions for your product, put it all together, arm yourself with proof of your solution's superiority, consider your initial pricing structure, and you'll be ready to take your narrative to the world.

CHAPTER 3

Sales Materials Basics: What You Need to Sell & How to Build it

Now that you've baked your narrative, it's time to create the materials to communicate it to potential customers. We'll focus on the essentials—slides for sales presentations, email templates and phone scripts for prospecting, sales-demo scripting, and basic video content.

A NOTE ON PRODUCTION VALUE & SPEED

Don't fall into the trap of thinking everything must be perfect before presenting to customers. Speed is key in early-stage sales. Opt for "good enough to persuade" over "perfect." Ten rough screencasts explaining your features will be more impactful than one polished explainer video.

SALES PRESENTATIONS

Start with slides. They're versatile, visual, and expected by customers. A good presentation sets up a great demo.

Structuring Your Deck for Extensibility

Build your deck to correspond with your sales narrative steps. Start with a minimum viable product—one slide for each step, with bullet points. As you evolve, break sections into "sub-chapters" with more detailed slides for each value proposition.

Production Value of Your Slides

Don't let lack of flashiness block content creation. Start with stark slides and impactful content. Basic improvements like a simple template, consistent colors, and your logo can boost production value. Use Upwork designers for polish after creating content yourself.

Content Management and Deployment

Maintain a master slide deck as a repository, from which you can produce sales-ready versions. Save copies of each iteration to track changes.

Customization Mindset

Tailor your presentation to each customer's pain points. Use specific customer information in your slides and demo to show exactly how your solution applies to them.

Remember, the goal is to communicate business meaning effectively. Flash without a valid narrative is worse than no flash at all. Focus on content first, then gradually improve aesthetics and customization.

Section-Specific Slide Deck Notes

1. The Problem and Who Has It: Start with this to quickly identify if your solution fits the prospect's needs. Include validators like industry stats and press clippings. For example, TalentBin used slides showing the low unemployment rate for technical, creative, and healthcare talent.

2. Cost of the Problem: Demonstrate the problem's financial impact. Use metrics that can be applied to the prospect's business, like cost per rep or foregone revenue. For a sales CRM solution, highlight the opportunity cost of lost deals per rep or how increased efficiency can add additional deals per month.

3. Existing Solutions and Their Challenges: Carefully address competition, focusing on how you're different and better. Group existing solutions into buckets if necessary. For TalentBin, this meant addressing LinkedIn Recruiter's challenges in technical recruiting, such as incomplete profiles and decreasing effectiveness of InMails.

4. **What Has Changed:** Explain market changes that created the opportunity for your solution. This ensures the prospect understands the context. TalentBin used a timeline slide to show the evolution of online talent search, from resume databases to professional networks to web-wide talent search.

5. **How Your Solution Works:** Include a conceptual visualization of your solution. Compare it to familiar solutions if helpful. TalentBin used diagrams showing how they aggregated candidate data from across the web into unified profiles, contrasting this with LinkedIn's approach.

6. **Quantitative/Qualitative Proof of a Better Solution:** Answer "Why you?" and "Why now?" Present proof bucketed by value proposition, demonstrating impact on relevant metrics. For example, show how your solution improves specific KPIs like talent pool richness or candidate responsiveness.

Remember to tailor these sections to your specific product and market. Use visuals, diagrams, and examples to clarify complex concepts. The goal is to build a compelling case for your solution, demonstrating why it's superior to existing options and why the prospect should act now.

When addressing existing solutions, be prepared to skip these slides if you discover the prospect doesn't use them. Always tie your points back to the prospect's business metrics and pain points.

In the "What Has Changed" section, use this as an opportunity to check the prospect's understanding. If they're not following, take the time to ensure they grasp the market context before moving on.

For the "How Your Solution Works" section, consider using comparison diagrams. TalentBin, for instance, explained their solution as "LinkedIn Recruiter, but where the database is the entire Internet," which resonated well with clients familiar with LinkedIn's tools.

Quantitative Proof

Present both granular and high-level proof of your solution's superiority. For TalentBin, granular proof included search-results superiority and contact-information density, while high-level proof showed reduced time to hire and cost per hire. Clear presentation is crucial as you're competing not just against similar solutions, but for the prospect's overall time and budget.

Examples from TalentBin included:

- Superior search results compared to industry standards
- Enhanced candidate responsiveness via drip-marketing
- Recruiter time savings via automation

Qualitative Proof

Complement quantitative data with qualitative proof, typically in the form of customer success stories. These should align with your value propositions. Pro tip—offer to write testimonials for early customers, making it easy for them to approve.

Company-centric Proof Points

Include third-party validations like press or analyst coverage. A "logos" slide can show prospects they'll be in good company. Ensure it represents all your target segments.

Why This Will Be So Easy

Address implementation concerns by showing how easy it is to get started and the ongoing support you provide. This counters potential objections about time investment.

Pricing

Include a clear pricing slide. If you have multiple options, present the one you want to push, keeping alternatives for follow-up discussions.

Appendices

Use appendices for information that's not universally relevant. This keeps your main presentation focused while allowing you to quickly address specific questions when they arise.

Deck for Presenting, Deck for Sending

Maintain two versions of your deck—a comprehensive one for live presentations and an abridged version for sending afterward. The latter serves as a reminder of key points and a teaser for other stakeholders. Using tools like DocSend or Showpad allows you to track prospect interactions with your materials, providing insights into their level of interest.

Remember, the sent deck isn't a substitute for additional presentations to other stakeholders, but a tool to drive further engagement.

OUTREACH MATERIALS

After finalizing your deck, focus on creating opportunities to present it. This involves crafting effective emails and phone scripts.

Email Templates

Email templates are crucial for both inbound inquiries and targeted outreach. They should encapsulate your narrative and drive recipients towards a presentation or demo.

Cold Outreach Emails

Create templates that:

1. Address specific pain points
2. Use customized subject lines
3. Include "click targets" (e.g., demo videos)
4. Maintain a conversational tone
5. Have strong calls to action

Example cold outreach email:

> Subject: Hiring Ruby devs? That is NOT easy.
>
> Hi [Name],
>
> I noticed [Company] is hiring Ruby developers. As you know, that's incredibly challenging in this market.
>
> We've developed a solution that's helping companies like Uber and Airbnb find 5-10x more Ruby developer candidates. How? By aggregating developers' public activity across 50+ sites like Github, StackOverflow, and Quora.
>
> Would you be open to a quick demo to see if this could help your hiring efforts?
>
> Best,
>
> [Your Name]

Consider building a multi-week drip campaign to cover different aspects of your solution over time.

Warm Outreach Emails

When using an intermediary:

1. Contact the intermediary first
2. Provide a forwardable email template
3. Include a clear call to action
4. Use email tracking
5. Follow up directly if needed

Phone and Voicemail Scripts

Develop scripts that:

- Can be delivered in 30-90 seconds
- Encapsulate your core narrative
- Include reaction permutations

Example cold-calling script:

> Hi [Name], this is [Your Name] from [Your Company].
>
> We help recruiting agencies like yours recover lost revenue from unreported hires. Our data shows that, on average, 8% of placements go unreported.
>
> For example, we recently helped [Similar Agency] recover $400,000 in a single quarter from placements they didn't know about.
>
> Do you have a few minutes this week to see how this might work for your agency?

Voicemail script:

> Hi [Name], it's [Your Name] from [Your Company]. I'm reaching out because we've developed a tool that's helping agencies like yours recover significant lost revenue from unreported hires.
>
> I'll follow up with an email, but if you're interested in learning how we recently helped [Similar Agency] recover $400,000 in a single quarter, give me a call back at [Your Number].
>
> Thanks, and I hope to speak with you soon.

Remember to iterate on these materials as your solution evolves. Store them in a centralized repository for easy access and updates.

DEMO SCRIPTS

Before diving into the presentation process, it's crucial to plan the content you'll demonstrate when prospects agree to a formal sales presentation. Your demo should align with your narrative and build upon the framing presented in your sales deck.

Customization

Customizing your demo for each prospect is key. At minimum, understand their business context and use it to guide your demo. For example, at TalentBin, we'd research the prospect's hiring needs beforehand:

> *I know from your careers page that you're hiring iOS developers in Philadelphia. Let me show you how TalentBin can help with that.*

For more advanced customization, consider using the prospect's actual data in the demo. HIRABL, for instance, analyzes the prospect's candidate submission data before the demo, showing real missed fees:

> We've found about 25 missed fees from your last two years of data. At $20,000 per placement, that's $400,000 in missed fees. Would you like to purchase the product to start collecting that?

Example Demo Script

Here's an abridged version of TalentBin's demo script, focusing on the "Search" and "Qualify" sections:

Search

> Let's search for Ruby engineers in Dallas. We can use our Job Req Translator to automatically extract relevant terms from your job posting. We've found about 8,000 results, compared to LinkedIn's 1,100. That's seven times more potential candidates!

Qualify

> Let's look at Natalie's profile. We've aggregated her GitHub, Stack Overflow, Meetup, Twitter, LinkedIn, and Facebook profiles.
>
> Click on 'Ruby' in her interest viewer. See how involved she is with Ruby? She follows Ruby repositories, mentions it in her Twitter bio, attends Ruby Meetups, and answers Ruby questions on Stack Overflow.
>
> Her LinkedIn profile is gone, but we still have all this valuable information about her skills and interests.

Remember to tailor your demo to your product's natural workflow and focus on how it solves your prospects' pain points. A successful demo will have prospects saying, "That's awesome" or "You have no idea how much this will help me with XYZ."

VIDEO MATERIALS

Video is a powerful tool for accelerating appointment setting in early-stage sales. It provides rich communication that surpasses email templates or other visual exhibits.

MVP Overview Video

The goal is to sell the prospect on the next step—getting on the phone for discovery, presentation, and a demo. It doesn't have to be perfect, just existing is key. Here's how to create one:

1. Put together a shortened sales presentation and demo.
2. Record it on your laptop while narrating (use tools like Camtasia, Snagit, or QuickTime).
3. Upload to YouTube for mobile-friendliness and trust.

Example: TalentBin's healthcare vertical overview video (https://drive.google.com/file/d/0ByAYCl_pIYjWQ1VzdHhOWGRWQzQ/view?usp=sharing)

Explainer Videos

These are more abstract presentations of the sales narrative, often animated and professionally produced. They're great for website visitors and as prospecting email collateral. Aim for under two minutes. Don't delay other video content while waiting for a perfect explainer. Example: TalentBin's explainer video (https://www.youtube.com/watch?v=Jvjpj88f-LU)

OTHER TYPES OF COLLATERAL

While there are many types of marketing collateral (PDFs, webinars, infographics, etc.), focus on the basics first. Treat collateral as "features" in your go-to-market, weighing their value against time and cost.

One-off Requests

When prospects request specific collateral, consider if existing materials already address their needs before creating something new.

On-Demand Collateral

Highly customized, prospect-specific content can accelerate sales conversations. Examples:

- Screenshots of search results (TalentBin example: "Hi Jeff, see these iOS developer search results for Boston—4 times what you would find on LinkedIn!")
- Short, targeted video walk-throughs (5-minute Jing recordings of specific searches)

Consider what customized content would make your prospects pay attention and convince decision-makers.

With these materials—a smart deck, outreach templates, a prospect-focused demo, and a growing video library—you're equipped to start selling and iterating based on prospect feedback.

CHAPTER 4

Early Prospecting: Finding Your First Customers

Now that you've prepared your materials, it's time to find prospects. Your goal is to proactively identify 50-100 potential clients with the specific pain point your solution addresses.

IDEAL CUSTOMER PROFILE: WHAT DOES YOUR PROSPECT LOOK LIKE?

One of the biggest mistakes founders make is trying to sell to people who don't have the problem their solution solves. This wastes time and resources, and can lead to unhappy customers who don't get value from your product.

Instead of prioritizing availability or existing relationships, focus on identifying companies and individuals with the business pain your product resolves. This approach is more effective and respects everyone's time.

SO WHO DOES HAVE MY PAIN POINT?

Your ideal customer profile should be based on your sales narrative and boiled down to specific characteristics. For example, TalentBin's ideal customer might be: "An account with five technical recruiters, twenty open technical hires (including iOS, Java, and Android roles), and uses LinkedIn Recruiter."

For Immediately, a mobile email client and CRM tool, it might be: "An account using Gmail, Salesforce, and Marketo, with fifty sales reps across the US, selling software averaging $50k, and a Sales Operations Manager reporting to the VP of Sales."

These profiles include both outwardly identifiable characteristics and those that may require discovery during initial conversations.

Remember, your goal is to identify potential demand for your solution based on these characteristics. While tools for finding this information may change, the core concept of identifying prospects based on their outward-facing characteristics remains key to successful prospecting.

Finding Outwardly Available Data

When prospecting, you can start with people or companies. For account sourcing based on people, LinkedIn's premium talent solutions are hard to beat, especially for job title information. Remember, though, that your ideal customer is typically an organization, not an individual.

For account sourcing based on company characteristics, consider:

1. Traditional providers: Dun & Bradstreet, Hoover's, Salesforce's Data.com
2. Modern variants: DiscoverOrg, ZoomInfo
3. Small business sources: Yelp, Radius, InfoUSA's Salesgenie, Google Maps
4. Technology-focused: BuiltWith, Datanyze, Datafox, SimilarWeb, HGData, Wappalyzer
5. Self-reported information: DiscoverOrg, Siftery, RainKing

Hiring information can also be valuable for account sourcing. Check company websites, job boards, and platforms like Glassdoor or LinkedIn.

Don't rely solely on marketing list providers, as they're often outdated and poorly modeled. Manual prospecting is valuable for understanding your ideal customer profile better.

Getting Data That Isn't Outwardly Discoverable

Some important characteristics may not be publicly available. For instance, TalentBin found that an organization's use of LinkedIn Recruiter was a great indicator of fit, but this information wasn't public. In these cases:

1. Look for correlating public information (e.g., premium LinkedIn Company Page, job postings on LinkedIn)
2. Ask prospects directly during inbound lead capture or phone calls
3. Use content and inbound marketing to attract prospects with these hidden characteristics

For your initial 100 targets, focus on direct prospecting combined with discovery questions for key characteristics that aren't readily observable.

Rolling Up The Demand Signifiers

When creating your ideal customer profile, consider both minimum requirements and demand magnitude. This helps prioritize prospects and understand potential deal sizes. Develop a "customer attractiveness" scoring algorithm based on relevant factors for your solution.

ACCOUNT SOURCING: PUTTING IT INTO PRACTICE

Prospect Data Management

Use a Google Sheet initially to manage prospect data. Include columns for key information and metadata that can be used for targeted outreach.

Rabbits, Deer, or Elephants?

Target "deer"—mid-sized organizations with enough pain to adopt new solutions but small enough to make quick decisions. Avoid "elephants" (large, slow-moving organizations) and "rabbits"—too small to provide significant value.

Geography

Start with accounts in your own geography for easier communication and potential on-site visits.

Account First? Contact First?

Choose your starting point (people or company) based on your solution's qualifying characteristics and available data sources.

People-centric Sourcing

Use LinkedIn to search for relevant titles, constraining by geography and company size. Capture account names and demand signifiers.

Company-centric Sourcing

Use company-specific metadata (e.g., industry, size) to find potential accounts. LinkedIn's Company search function can be helpful for this approach.

Remember to tailor your sourcing strategy to your specific solution and target market. Consider what data sources and approaches would be most relevant for identifying your ideal customers.

POINT(S)-OF-CONTACT DISCOVER: WHO WILL BE EXCITED ABOUT YOUR SOLUTION?

After identifying promising accounts, focus on finding the right decision-makers to engage. Look for individuals responsible for solving the pain your solution addresses, with decision-making authority and budgetary control.

Identifying Decision-Makers

1. Use LinkedIn or similar platforms to search for relevant titles within target accounts.
2. Consider a "cascading" approach, capturing multiple potential points of contact (e.g., VP of Sales, Director of Sales Operations, Sales Operations Manager).
3. Use Boolean searches to find relevant titles efficiently.

Complementary Decision-Makers

Consider targeting internal customers of the primary decision-maker (e.g., CTO for a recruiting solution, VP of Sales for a sales operations tool). These individuals can be valuable allies or provide referrals.

Contact Information

1. Focus on obtaining email addresses for initial outreach.
2. Use tools like Apollo, Lusha, or LeadIQ to find email addresses associated with LinkedIn profiles.
3. Collect phone numbers as well, especially for local businesses.

Warm Introductions

Look for shared connections on LinkedIn or Facebook that could provide a warm introduction to your target contact.

Bottom-Up Prospecting

While more advanced, consider targeting individual users to build support from within the organization.

Now that you have a list of 50-100 prospect accounts with relevant contacts, it's time to put your sales narrative and materials to use. Go sell!

CHAPTER 5

Prospect Outreach & Demo Appointment Setting

Now that you have your list of targeted accounts and contacts, it's time to start selling. This chapter focuses on "outreach and engagement" with the goal of setting appointments.

STAGES OF THE SALES CYCLE

The main stages of the sales cycle includes:

1. Outreach and engagement
2. Pitching
3. Closing

As a founder, you'll be handling all these stages initially. This "evangelical sales" approach combines product management, product marketing, and sales.

SETTING YOURSELF UP FOR SUCCESS

Management and Early CRM

While a full CRM like Salesforce might be overkill to start, you need a system to track prospects and interactions. Options include:

- Google Sheets
- Beginner CRMs (Pipedrive, Close.io, Insightly, Hubspot CRM)

Eventually, you'll likely transition to Salesforce; it's just a question of when.

Materials and Personalization

Prepare:

- List of prospects with relevant metadata
- Outreach emails with supporting collateral
- Phone scripts

Personalize your outreach to stand out from generic sales pitches.

EMAILING

Email is powerful for outreach when done correctly.

- Use pre-qualified prospects and their email addresses
- Create multiple email templates to "drip" your message over time
- Keep emails concise, focusing on one main point per email
- Use a conversational, calm tone
- Avoid excessive formatting or exclamation points

Manual Email and Instrumentation

Use email tracking tools (e.g., Yesware, Tout, Sidekick) to monitor opens and clicks. This data helps you gauge interest and time follow-ups effectively. Consider lightweight CRMs or SDR tools that integrate email functionality and tracking.

Mass Mail and Drip Marketing

Drip marketing involves sending a series of emails over time, nurturing prospects towards conversion. It's like driving a brand-new Tesla compared to the mid-2000s Camaro of manual emailing.

Key points:

- Use tools like Outreach, Salesloft, PersistIQ, MixMax, or Sendbloom for lightweight drip marketing
- Personalize initial outreach for higher response rates (up to 12% vs. 5% for unpersonalized)
- Create a "single-serving drip-marketing campaign" with highly customized
  initial outreach
- Leverage social context (LinkedIn, Twitter) to build rapport (e.g., mention their alma mater or recent tweet)
- Time emails strategically (e.g., 10am Tuesday, 6-7am, 7-8pm) to avoid busy
  inbox times
- Response rates often peak at the second email (18%), then hold steady through
  the fifth
- Add a "breaking up" email at the end to prompt action

Remember, it's not spam if you've targeted well and your message is relevant and valuable. Good prospecting and messaging make you stand out from the sea of terrible, irrelevant outreach.

CALLING

Don't fear cold-calling. It's a rich way to communicate if done right. Think of it as helping qualified contacts solve a problem they have.

Attempting Contact

- Time calls based on prospect's daily rhythm (e.g., early morning or late afternoon for office workers, 2-3pm for restaurants between lunch and dinner)
- Use email tracking to inform call timing (e.g., call soon after an email open)

- For SMBs without clear contacts, prepare a simple value proposition for gatekeepers (e.g., "I'd like to discuss how Groupon can make him twenty thousand dollars in one day.")
- Follow the "10am hour" across time zones to maximize connect rates

Gatekeepers and Directories

- Try dial-by-name directories when available
- With human gatekeepers, be pleasant and respectful—differentiate yourself from pushy sales reps
- Provide a short pitch on why your offering is relevant (e.g., "Twenty thousand in a single day. Sounds great, right?")
- Ask for voicemail if unable to connect directly
- Try to get the direct number for future reference

Voice Mails

- Keep them short, personalized, and benefit-focused
- Always pair voicemails with emails
- Consider that voicemails may be forwarded as audio emails
- Avoid tricks like fake "returning your call" messages—stick to straight-forward, email-like voicemails

Live Messages

- Avoid having gatekeepers take messages; prefer leaving voicemail or getting an email address
- If necessary, provide a simple, compelling message for the gatekeeper to pass along
- Try to get the decision-maker's email or offer to send details to the gatekeeper's email
- Suggest a combination approach: "Note that Pete called about making twenty thousand in a day, here's my number, and the details are in the voicemail."

By combining these strategies, you can effectively reach out to prospects and increase your chances of setting up meaningful conversations. Remember, the goal is to demonstrate that you've done your research and that your solution is relevant to their situation. With practice, you'll become more comfortable with these outreach methods and start seeing results.

Making Contact

When you actually reach a prospect, remember—you're not selling the product, you're selling a brief appointment to discuss their pain points and potential solutions.

Success

If they agree to a follow-up:

- Get calendar availability immediately
- Aim for 2-3 days out, not more than a week
- Gather additional contact info
- Consider involving other relevant team members

Hot Transfers

If they want to talk now:

- Treat it as a "demo lite"
- Set expectations and use the time for discovery
- Sell a full demo for later

Rejection

- Don't take it as "never," but as "not now"
- Offer to table the discussion for a more appropriate time
- Send a follow-up email reiterating your value proposition

Objection

Objections are opportunities to engage and make a better case. Common objections and responses:

1. "Call me later"—Offer a quick 30-second qualification now to avoid future irrelevant outreach
2. "I don't have budget"—Pivot to learning about their processes, not selling
3. "Just send me some information"—Offer a quick qualification to ensure relevance before sending personalized info
4. "We already use [competitor]"—Congratulate them on addressing the problem, then highlight your unique benefits
5. "Do you have [specific feature]?"—Use their interest to schedule a full demo
6. "How much does it cost?"—Explain that pricing depends on value, and suggest a demo to assess fit
7. "I can't make that decision"—Determine if they're the wrong contact or deflecting. If wrong contact, ask who the right person is. If deflecting, reassure that you're just seeking to understand their processes.

Remember to record objections and your responses for future reference and team training.

SETTING UP THE APPOINTMENT

Meeting Invites

When setting up appointments, always send a calendar invite with all relevant details. For early-stage customers, I prefer in-person meetings. If digital, use tools like Zoom or join.me. Include location details, a brief agenda, and a descriptive title in the invite. Consider adding "teaser" material to excite prospects.

Time Blocking

Block 15-30 minutes before and after appointments for preparation and follow-up. Treat each appointment seriously, as it represents significant potential revenue.

Reminders

Use calendar reminders (15 minutes before) and email reminders (early morning of the meeting) to ensure attendance. Reminder emails also help set expectations and tease content.

CADENCING: PUTTING IT ALL TOGETHER

Implement a series of outreach actions (emails, calls, voicemails) over time, known as a "cadence." Alternate between methods, adjusting based on your content and results. Use contextual data to prioritize prospects showing interest.

REFERRAL PROSPECTING

Leverage social networks like LinkedIn and Facebook to discover connections for referrals. Focus on qualified accounts that have the pain your solution solves.

Connection Discovery

- Connect with everyone in your organization, investors, and advisors on LinkedIn and Facebook.
- Review profiles of decision-maker prospects to find shared connections.
- Reach out to potential referrers, explaining who you want to contact and why.

Contact Outreach

- Qualify organizations to ensure they're a fit for your solution.

- Send introduction request emails to referrers, making it easy for them to forward.
- Use email tracking to monitor forwarded emails.
- Follow up quickly when introduced, moving referrers to BCC.

Consider using software like Teamable for more scalable referral prospecting. Remember to thank your referrers, possibly with gift cards for their time and successful introductions.

INBOUND LEAD CAPTURE & RESPONSE PREVIEW

Your outbound appointment-setting efforts will generate inbound interest. People will visit your website after reading your emails or hearing your voicemails. It's crucial to capture and respond to this interest effectively.

Lead Capture Basics

1. Provide an easy way for website visitors to express interest.
2. Start simple: a "Request a demo" button with a mailto: link to sales@yourcompany.com.
3. Consider pre-filling email subject and content for convenience.
4. For a more advanced approach, use a Google Form.

Notification System

Set up email notifications for lead requests. I prefer automatically foldered notifications that bold when new leads arrive.

Quick Response

Respond to inbound leads as fast as possible. Don't let their interest cool—capitalize on it immediately and set the appointment.

Remember, B2B sales rarely close in one call. It's a stepwise process starting with identification and progressing to a formal evaluation. Use these thoughtful, methodical outreach strategies to book appointments consistently, setting yourself up for success in the demo phase.

CHAPTER 6

Early Inbound Lead Capture & Response

I don't want to delve too deep into inbound marketing here. When you're just starting your go-to-market strategy, it's unlikely that people know who you are or what you do. This is especially challenging when selling innovative solutions—if no one knows they have the problem you solve, they won't be searching for you online.

Inbound marketing—creating SEO-optimized content like blog posts, tweets, and infographics—is a more advanced form of lead generation that we'll cover later. It's typically not appropriate for very early-stage go-to-market efforts. You'd be producing content for an audience that isn't looking for it yet.

However, you still need a minimum viable inbound lead capture process to capitalize on your outbound appointment-setting activity. I call this "outbound inbound," where your targeted outreach drives qualified prospects to your website. These leads are often the strongest, as you know you're targeting qualified accounts.

Standard inbound leads are a double-edged sword. They have high "intent," as prospects are actively asking you to sell to them. The downside is that the requester might not be well-informed about what qualifies them for your solution.

INBOUND LEAD QUALIFICATION

As we discussed in the Prospecting chapter, focus on potential customers with the characteristics required for success with your solution—namely, the business pain points you solve and the staff who would use your solution. If they don't meet these criteria, it's better to funnel them away politely than waste time on unqualified leads.

INBOUND LEAD CAPTURE FORMS

First, you need a way to capture inbound leads in a structured format. We previously mentioned setting up a sales@yourcompanyname.com inbox as an early solution. While better than nothing, it makes capturing relevant demand signifiers difficult.

As soon as possible, replace the email link with a prominent "Request Demo" button on your homepage. This should lead to a form that captures structured data. Don't be subtle—if someone is eager to talk to you, make it extremely easy for them.

Use a form tool like Google Forms, Wufoo, or Typeform to start. Ensure it works on mobile, as that's where much of your email outreach will be read. Many CRMs offer lead capture forms that route leads directly into the CRM and can provide automated responses.

What information should you capture? Resist the urge to ask for too much. Focus on qualification information and contact details. At minimum, collect:

1. First name, last name
2. Company name, title
3. Email address, phone number
4. Minimum viable demand signifiers you can't easily find elsewhere

For example, at TalentBin, we didn't ask how many recruiters a company had (easy to find on LinkedIn) but did ask about their hiring plans for software engineers (not publicly available). Think about what qualification signifiers are crucial for your solution and not observable externally.

Best Practices

1. Add "Request Demo" calls-to-action on your homepage and other relevant pages.
2. Merchandise your demo request form in outreach emails, perhaps in the footer.
3. Include a phone number on your form for those who prefer verbal communication. Don't worry about unwanted calls—your bigger problem is people not caring about you, rather than too much inbound interest.
4. Ensure your form works on mobile devices.
5. Consider using CRM lead capture forms for direct routing and automated responses.

Remember, at this early stage, make it as easy as possible for interested prospects to get in touch. You can always refine your process later if you start receiving too many unqualified leads.

CHAPTER 7

Pitching: Preparation, Presentation, Demos & Objections

You've probably been thinking, "Pete, when do we get down to the actual selling?" Now's the time, friend. We've covered getting your story straight, documenting it, finding accounts, and getting demos on calendars. All of that is "selling," but now we're diving into the mechanics of executing your sales presentation, demo, and closing business.

THE GOAL OF PITCHING

Pitching is the process of commercial persuasion, ending in a sale. It's about convincing prospects that:

1. They have a significant business pain
2. Your solution will solve it
3. They'll see a return on investment by implementing it now
4. They need to deal with this now, not later

This isn't typically a one-call close, especially for complex solutions. It may take multiple steps and meetings, involving various people within the target organization.

NEW-TECHNOLOGY SALES PERSUASION FORMULA

Potential Value x Value Comprehension x Belief = Likelihood and Magnitude of Sale

Maximize each term:

- Target accounts with the greatest need for your solution
- Ensure comprehension through effective presentation and materials
- Boost believability via proof points, demonstrations, and even pilots

Even if you can't maximize all terms, focusing on high-pain organizations and ensuring comprehension can often overcome skepticism.

INSIDE OR OUTSIDE SALES?

For early-stage sales, prioritize in-person meetings when possible. The increased fidelity of communication, insights from face-to-face exchanges, and trust-building outweigh the efficiency of digital presentations. This is why we focused on prospects in your geographical vicinity earlier.

As you scale, you can reassess based on:

- Solution complexity
- Average deal size
- Efficiency needs

You might end up with a blend, where smaller customers are addressed via telepresence and larger ones in-person.

PRE-CALL PLANNING

Preparation is crucial. Block 15 minutes before each meeting for pre-call planning. For outside sales, include travel time in your calendar, aiming to arrive 30 minutes early.

Key areas to research:

1. Pain Points & "Size of Prize"
   - Identify outward signifiers of demand
   - Determine potential sale size (e.g., number of users, seats)
2. Complementary/Competitive Products & Capacity to Pay
   - Use tools like Datanyze and BuiltWith to understand their tech stack
   - Check funding situation or financial health
3. Potential Users
   - Use LinkedIn to identify who would use your solution
4. Stakeholders & Influencers
   - Identify decision-makers, their bosses, and internal customers
   - Understanding the organizational structure helps you navigate the sale
5. Customization Information
   - Gather info to personalize your presentation (e.g., specific job openings for a recruiting tool)
6. Conversational Guides/Icebreakers
   - Use LinkedIn, Twitter for personal interests, shared connections
   - Avoid politics and religion
7. Known Unknowns
   - Note what you couldn't find to ask during discovery

Stated Pitch Goal

Establish a clear goal for each call. This could be:

- Winning consideration for purchase
- Driving towards a second call with decision-makers
- Partnering with an internal sponsor

Pre-Call Attitude

Get in the zone before your call. Project confidence in your solution and your recommendations. Consider:

- Standing during calls
- Doing light exercise to energize yourself
- Using a standing desk if possible

Remember, thorough preparation can significantly boost your win rate. If proper preparation raises your win rate from 15% to 25% on a $20,000 average contract, you've just made $2,000 with fifteen minutes of work. Don't skimp on this crucial step—it's not optional, it's essential for success.

PITCH MATERIALS & CONCEPTS

Tools and Materials

Be prepared for both on-site and digital pitches.

For on-site pitches:

- Bring a laptop with your sales deck and demo materials.
- Pack all necessary projector connectors (keep them in a mesh bag for easy access).
- Consider bringing a mini projector for backup.
- Have a personal hotspot to avoid Wi-Fi issues.
- Bring a lab notebook for note-taking.

For digital pitches:

- Use reliable screen-sharing software (e.g., join.me, Showpad, DocSend) that doesn't require downloads.
- Have good quality earbuds or a headset.
- Keep your lab notebook handy for notes.

Always have an "offline proof" version of your demo with key screens pre-populated in your browser.

Pitch Format

Follow a consistent format:

1. Quick pleasantries
2. Discovery
3. Slide-based presentation
4. Live demo
5. Success proof points
6. Pricing and commercial discussion

This format builds the best case for your solution. As you scale, consider separating discovery and presentation into two calls, but start with combined sessions for richer conversations.

Who Are You Talking To?

Tailor your message to three personas:

1. End users:
   - Focus on making their jobs easier and career progress.
   - Emphasize personal benefits over ROI arguments.
2. First-line managers:
   - Highlight ROI and team efficiency.
   - Address budget concerns and impact on internal customers.
3. Second-level managers/CXOs:
   - Emphasize top-line business value for the entire organization.
   - Focus on how your solution impacts company-wide metrics and valuation.

Be prepared to speak different "languages" when multiple personas are in the same meeting.

PITCH INTRODUCTION

Start with rapport building, then transition to business:

- Use pre-gathered information for hypercharged rapport building.
- Keep it brief (2-3 minutes) to avoid wearing thin.
- Transition from personal to professional topics as a segue.

Discovery

Allocate 5-10 minutes for discovery at the start of your pitch. Key points:

- Explain the purpose of discovery to the prospect as a benefit to them.
- Use qualification frameworks like BANT (Budget, Authority, Need, Timeline), ANUM (Authority, Need, Urgency, Money), or ChAMP (Challenges, Authority, Money, Prioritization).
- Validate pre-gathered information and show you've done your homework.
- Ask leading questions based on known information.
- Document your discovery questions for future use and refinement.

Focus on two main areas:

1. Pain and Urgency
    - Confirm the prospect has the business pain your solution solves.
    - Understand the magnitude of the pain and previous solution attempts.
    - Explore downstream business implications of not solving the pain.
    - Tie questions to your solution's features.

        Example (for TalentBin): *I saw a few technical roles on your careers site. Over the next twelve months, how many software engineering positions do you expect to fill? What proportion of your total hires will this be?*

> *When you think about your current technical hiring process, would you consider it easy? Do you find job postings insufficient for getting the applicant flow you want?*
>
> *Have you had to do passive-candidate recruiting, for instance via LinkedIn? How's the responsiveness to LinkedIn outreach? Do you find yourself searching for personal email addresses to improve response rates?*

2. Team, Authority, and Commercials

   - Identify potential users in the organization and their specialties.
   - Determine decision-makers and the purchasing process.
   - Understand budget cycles and discretionary spending.
   - Explore past purchases of similar solutions.

   Example questions: *Who in your organization makes decisions about purchasing solutions like ours? Is there a formal evaluation period for this type of tool, or is there discretionary budget available?*

Remember, discovery helps qualify prospects, uncover valuable information, and demonstrates your commitment to understanding their needs. It's crucial for a productive pitch and down-funnel process. Even if a prospect doesn't have a set budget (common for innovative solutions), focus on the magnitude of the problem and the urgency to solve it.

If discovery reveals the prospect isn't qualified, politely end the conversation to respect both parties' time. However, if the pain exists and there's potential for a sale, use the information gathered to tailor your pitch and increase your chances of success.

PRESENTATION, DEMO, AND ASKING FOR THE SALE

After discovery, you'll shift from primarily consuming information to both consuming and communicating. You'll still be asking questions and eliciting feedback, but now you'll be presenting your sales narrative through slides, presentation, and demo scripting.

Overarching Guidelines

1. Repetition: Don't fear repeating key points. Your audience is new to this topic, so reinforce major messages throughout your pitch. Connect various parts of your presentation back to these key points to ensure they stick.

    - Validate attention and understanding:
    - In person, observe their focus. Are they looking at you or their phone?
    - On calls, ask confirming questions like "Can you see this on the slide?"
    - Give permission to not understand. Say things like, "It's okay if you haven't heard of these before. Many are fairly new!"

2. Ask specific questions related to pain points or features. For example, "Do you find your field reps have this same issue?" or "Can you see how this automation would reduce manual follow-up?"

3. Rolling discovery: Continue learning about the prospect's needs throughout the presentation. If you're presenting pain point slides, ask if they encounter these challenges. Use their responses to tailor your pitch and demonstrate how your solution addresses their specific issues.

4. Build agreement: Regularly seek the prospect's agreement on pain points, solutions, and features. Use leading questions to surface agreement or disagreement. Each "yes" builds alignment towards a purchase decision.

5. Pacing and pausing: Resist the urge to speed through familiar content. Speak deliberately and pause for questions, especially on phone calls where non-verbal cues are absent.

6. Customization: Use your research to personalize the pitch. Skip irrelevant slides or features, and focus on what matters most to this prospect. For instance, if pitching to someone familiar with your industry, you might gloss over basic concepts and focus more on your unique differentiators.

7. Micro-contracts: Set clear expectations and next steps throughout the process. For example: "It seems you believe this solution can help. To progress, we need to involve Jeff. Shall we schedule that meeting now?" If you make a micro-contract, restate it at the start of the next meeting: "Jeff, Susan and I met last week to discuss your challenges. We believe this is a worthwhile investment, but we need your validation before progressing to a commercial agreement. Does that align with your expectations?"

These micro-contracts keep you aligned with the prospect and help identify potential issues early. If a prospect diverges from their commitment, it's an early warning sign. You can then address it directly:

> *I'm confused. We agreed this solution makes sense for you, and our next step was to meet your CFO. But two meetings have been canceled. Can you confirm this is still a priority for your organization?*

Remember, your time is your most valuable resource in sales. There are thousands of potential prospects, but you only have 40-60 hours in your week. These techniques help ensure you're spending that time effectively, always knowing where you stand, and moving towards a successful sale.

Presentation and Demo Strategies

Presentation

I believe it's crucial to set the correct "mental model" before jumping into the product demo. Start by framing the problem you solve and how your solution helps. Avoid a one-way "show and tell" approach; instead, cultivate rich back-and-forth with the prospect.

Be explicit about your process: "Based on what you've shared, I think we're relevant to what you're doing at [company]. I'd like to share some slides to set the tone before we get into the live demo. Does that work for you?"

If the prospect isn't qualified, respectfully end the conversation: "I don't think we'll be super helpful in your efforts. We mainly help with [specific problem]. I'm happy to send materials, but I propose we conclude this call to respect your time."

Use slides to convey parts of your sales narrative that aren't best demonstrated live—pain points, current solution failures, and proof of your solution's effectiveness. Avoid getting into product features before the demo, unless a live demonstration isn't possible.

Demo

The demo shows how your product delivers on the promises made in the presentation. Customize it heavily for each prospect's needs.

1. Customization: If possible, use the prospect's actual data or materials. For example, Postini would filter a CIO's actual email traffic in real-time during demos.

2. Demo-Ready Data: If you can't use real data, ensure your demo data supports all necessary use cases. Avoid situations where you have to say, "Well, ignore that" or "Imagine if XYZ."

3. Focus on Relevant Features: Prioritize features that will be most compelling to your specific prospect. For instance, if selling Textio to someone frustrated with job description management, focus on templating and management features.

Remember to speak the "language" of your prospect and be prepared to cut optional parts to spend more time on high-priority features.

Proof Demonstration

After the demo, switch back to slides for proof points. This is where you show why your solution is a great investment, backed by ROI studies, customer examples, and other evidence. Don't skip this crucial step before closing.

Pricing and Asking for the Sale

This is often where founders make mistakes—by not presenting pricing or asking for the sale. Don't fear rejection; if your pitch is solid, you're justified in asking for part of the value you're creating.

Prospects often ask about pricing themselves. If they do, it's a good sign. If not, use a "trial close" to gauge interest before discussing price.

When presenting pricing, frame it in context of existing solutions or ROI. Start high, allowing room for negotiation. Present the price, explain the rationale, then wait for the reaction.

Asking for the Sale

Directly ask for the business with phrases like "Is this something you want to progress with?" or "Is there anything preventing us from getting you started as a customer?"

If they say yes, fantastic! Offer to create a proposal or send an order form. If no, it's usually an "I'm not sure" in disguise. Uncover and handle objections, then ask again.

Proposals

Proposals are for prospects who've expressed interest in buying. They allow you to present multiple options, potentially guiding the customer towards a more beneficial (for you) outcome. A good strategy is presenting three options:

1. Lowest tier at near list price
2. Middle tier (your target) with a compelling discount
3. Highest tier as a "stretch goal" with the best per-unit price

Include ROI projections to help your champion if they need to convince others internally. Deliver proposals using a templated PowerPoint to start, later moving to automated systems like Conga Composer or Octiv for efficiency. Remember, early on, focus on getting cash in the bank rather than worrying about cannibalization. Your goal is to close deals and grow your business.

HANDLING OBJECTIONS IN SALES

Most sales interactions won't result in an immediate yes or no. Instead, you'll encounter objections that need addressing before closing. Don't fear this process; it's where crucial sales work happens. Handling objections is about commercial persuasion, where you examine and surmount the barriers blocking your prospect from proceeding.

Be direct but respectful in your approach. This "respectful contentiousness" is particularly important in innovative technology sales, where you often need to challenge existing mindsets to popularize a new approach.

Generic Objections

Lack of Decision-Making Authority

If your prospect lacks authority, partner with them to sell to the next decision-maker. Ensure they're fully bought in first by asking, "Is the authority to make this decision the only thing blocking us from getting you started?" This helps uncover any lurking objections.

Take control of the process, treating it as another demo focused on business outcomes. Offer to set up the meeting with the decision-maker, saying something like, "I'm excited to work with you to help [decision-maker] understand how helpful this will be. I'd love to take point on setting an appointment so we can both present this."

We Don't Have a Need

This objection is concerning. Re-verify the need based on your discovery. If they truly don't need your product, improve your prospecting. If they do need it but don't see the value, dig deeper to uncover the real objection.

You might say, "I'm confused. Based on our earlier discussion, [recap need indicators]. Is this not the case?" If they confirm they don't have the need, learn from it for future prospecting. If their response is vague, probe further: "It appears to me that your organization definitely has the need for this, but perhaps there's something else blocking us from progressing?"

We're Happy with How We Do It Right Now/Fear of Change

Often, "we don't have a need" actually means "we're afraid to change." This is better because they've acknowledged the need; now you just need to show why they should adopt your solution.

Make the cost of not changing visible. Use quantitative and qualitative proof points from your sales materials.

For example:

> *By continuing your current approach, you're wasting $15,000-$40,000 a year. That's half a Recruiting Coordinator salary. Saving that would make you a hero to your CEO and VP of Engineering.*

Use qualitative arguments too, like industry trends and competitor adoption. Frame your solution as inevitable and the next logical step. Suggest that early adopters will look brilliant, while late adopters might look behind the times.

Address implementation fears by emphasizing your resources and support to ensure their success. Use customer success stories as proof. You might say, "Here are all the resources we have in place to ensure you capture the value we both agree is on the table for you. We will make you successful."

Remember, good discovery work gives you the information to handle objections effectively. Use what you've learned about the prospect's business realities to craft persuasive, tailored responses to their concerns.

Timing is Bad/We Have Higher Priorities

This objection indicates the prospect sees value but has other priorities. Address it by:

1. Reducing perceived implementation effort: "We have customer success specialists who can run daily webinars for your team. As you roll out your new ATS, you'll see even better ROI by mixing the two solutions."

2. Positioning your solution as a higher priority: Compare ROI with competing projects.

3. Using timing to your advantage: "If you buy now, I can give you fourteen months for the cost of twelve" or "You can buy now, and I'll start the contract in a month."

Price/Value

Price objections can be about value or just posturing for a discount. Determine which by asking, "What do you think would be a fair price?"

If it's about value, justify your pricing. For example:

> *Based on your submission volume, we quoted $40,000 for the year. We expect to catch 20 missed fees, driving $600,000 in revenue you'd otherwise miss. Given that, $40,000 is fair and will be nearly paid for by your first collected fee. Where is my analysis falling short?*

If the prospect has a legitimate rationale (e.g., lower average fees, partial use of functionality), consider exceptions or adjusting your pricing model.

When a prospect's best alternative differs significantly from the norm, adjust your ROI argument accordingly. For instance, if they're already doing manual checks, focus on automation benefits and expanded coverage.

These discussions are opportunities to learn what parts of your product are valuable to different customers. Early-stage, it's often better to get a deal done at a lower price if the prospect fits your ideal customer profile and will get value. Document the rationale for any pricing modifications in the contract for future reference and to avoid setting unintended precedents.

Don't sell to those who won't get value from your solution just because it's cheap. It wastes resources and leads to churn. This should be identified during discovery and qualification.

We Don't Have The Budget For This

Not having budget is often a failure of imagination. Your job is to help prospects find that budget. Here are some strategies:

1. Identify existing budgets for solving the problem you address. For example, with TalentBin, we'd look at budgets for recruiting agencies.

2. Consider budget transfers, like from payroll to tooling. For instance, Zendesk could reduce the need for new support agents, freeing up budget.

3. Tap into discretionary budgets. These are often for "experiments," so be prepared for smaller initial purchases.

4. Pursue one-off budgetary justifications. This can lead to larger deals and strategic discussions with C-level executives.

5. Offer creative financing solutions. For example, propose monthly payments at a higher total cost, which might motivate upfront payment to save money.

Remember, early-stage sales often require flexibility. Document any pricing modifications clearly in the contract to avoid setting unintended precedents.

I Need a Trial/I Need a Reference

When a prospect asks for a trial, they're really saying, "I need more proof." Address this by:

1. Asking what specific proof they need. Often, it's just customer success stories or ROI studies you already have.
2. Offering a guided demo for their team instead of an unstructured trial.
3. Providing a "ride-along" session where the prospect controls the product while you guide them.

Avoid unattended trials unless your product has strong self-serve onboarding. Instead, for larger deals, consider structured pilots with clear success metrics and prospect accountability.

For smaller deals, be firm, "We don't do unstructured trials because they don't lead to success. But I'm happy to do a guided session where you have control."

Remember, the goal is to provide proof while maintaining deal momentum and control. Tailor your approach to the deal size and prospect needs, always aiming to close efficiently.

HANDLING SPECIFIC OBJECTIONS AND DEMO FOLLOW-UP

Solution-Specific Objections

Solution-specific objections are opportunities to demonstrate expertise. Address them with quantitative and qualitative proof, ideally using prepared slides. For example, if selling HIRABL (software to catch missed recruiting fees), you might face concerns about fee collection. Counter with:

1. Aggregate client collection rates
2. Benefits of quick detection
3. Customer success tools for broaching the topic with clients

If an objection becomes frequent, consider including it proactively in your pitch. For instance, with TalentBin, we'd address candidate privacy concerns upfront: "Candidates are used to this and prefer it, as shown by our 3x email response rates compared to generic LinkedIn InMails."

Competition Objections

Use competitive objections to frame the broader conversation about your market. Don't just address the specific feature comparison; explain how your solution is superior across all relevant vectors.

For example, if asked about a competitor's code scoring feature, we'd say: "Great question! We use multiple data signals to understand candidates. But let's consider all aspects of talent search—discovery, qualification, contact information, and outreach. TalentBin uses the broadest set of sources, not just code repositories, to ensure you see all relevant engineers."

Prepare competitive framework slides for each major competitor, showing how you win in each category.

Generic Objection Flow Loop

For all objections:

1. Catch the objection
2. Identify the underlying question
3. Respond with proof and arguments
4. Validate understanding
5. Return to closing
6. Repeat until all objections are addressed or the prospect is ready to proceed

DEMO FOLLOW-UP & FURTHER MEETINGS

After a demo, clearly state the next action and get commitment. For example: "I'll send a contract for one seat via e-sign today, and you'll execute it. Correct?"

If further meetings are needed, calendar them immediately. Set specific follow-up appointments for information review or team discussions.

Always follow up with a summary email including:

1. Commitments made during the call
2. The "for sending" version of your sales presentation
3. Any appendix slides that were particularly important

Execute your follow-up actions quickly. Prospect commitments have a time decay rate; the faster you deliver, the more likely they are to follow through.

Continue this follow-up loop after every meeting until the opportunity is closed (won or lost).

PRACTICE & ITERATION

Nothing beats "live fire" drills with actual prospects to hone your sales skills. However, practice demos with objection handling can prepare you well. Use customer development interviewees, team members, or even your significant other for these practice sessions.

Remember, your pitch, demo, and objection responses aren't set in stone. Continuously improve them based on real-world performance. If something isn't working—like offering trials—don't hesitate to cut it out. Your pitch and down-funnel protocol should be viewed as a product you're constantly iterating. That said, raw activity drives success more than anything else. So get out there and start selling!

CHAPTER 8

Down Funnel Selling: Negotiation, Closing & Pipeline Management

NEGOTIATION AND CLOSING IN SALES

Negotiation is a normal part of the sales process, especially for complex or costly solutions. Anticipate it by building room into your initial pricing. Key levers include price, amount, contract duration, and payment terms.

Prioritize getting cash up front and longer contract terms. When negotiating, retreat one increment at a time. If a prospect asks for a discount, use it as an opportunity to improve other terms in your favor.

For example, if a customer wants a discount per seat, you might say, "We can provide better pricing if you buy more seats or extend the contract term." This way, you're giving them what they want while also moving a different lever in your favor.

Basic Negotiation Tactics

1. For cheaper per-unit price: Propose larger volume or longer contracts. Example: "If you commit to a two-year contract instead of one, we can reduce the per-seat price by 15%."

2. For lower total cost: Offer fewer units or shorter contracts at a higher per-unit price. Example: "We can meet your $10k budget with two seats for six months, or we can do two seats for a full year at $12k, which is a better value."

3. For shorter duration: Increase the per-time price significantly. Example: "A six-month contract would be $5k, compared to $7k for a full year, due to fixed onboarding costs."

4. For split payments: Raise pricing to reflect the increased risk and cost of capital. Example: "Annual upfront payment is $10k, while quarterly payments would total $12k for the year."

Creating Urgency

To encourage immediate execution:

- Offer the rest of the month free
- Mention limited customer success team slots
- State that current pricing is only valid for this month
- Suggest future price increases

For instance, "If you sign this week, I can throw in the rest of this month for free, giving you an extra three weeks of service."

Pushing Back Against Discounts

Use an authority backstop (e.g., "checking with the manager") to justify pushback. Remind the prospect of the fair value you're offering. Don't be afraid to explain that your pricing reflects real costs and the need to keep the business running.

You might say, "I understand you're looking for a lower price, but our engineers need to eat too. We've priced this fairly based on the value we provide and our costs."

Handling Competitors and Pricing

When facing competition:

1. Demonstrate superior value to justify higher prices. For example, at TalentBin, we showed how our automation features saved recruiters significant time compared to competitors.

2. If you can't justify higher prices, consider lowering them, but be sure to document why the competitor's additional features may be overkill or unlikely to be used.

3. If a prospect claims to have a lower competitor price, ask to see the proposal before matching or discounting. Say, "To justify any pricing changes, I'll need to see that competitor proposal. Can you share it with me?"

4. When offering to match a competitor's price, require immediate contract execution to avoid a bidding war. "I can match that price, but only if we can execute the contract today."

Remember, the goal is to close deals efficiently while maintaining profitability. Be flexible but strategic in your negotiations, always keeping in mind the value you provide and the costs you need to cover.

CLOSING DEALS & FOLLOW-UP

Close Winning

Don't celebrate too early. Run until the money's in the bank and the customer is up and running. Closing is just another step to nail, with more to follow.

Order Forms and Contracts

Act quickly to execute the contract. Use simple order forms with e-signature software. For example, at TalentBin, we used a straightforward order form with Adobe eSign, integrated with Salesforce.

Keep the legalese separate to avoid complications. Link to your Master Service Agreement (MSA) rather than attaching it to the order form. This approach reduces friction and speeds up the deal process.

If you encounter redlining, consider stating that your contract is non-negotiable. If that doesn't work, involve your corporate counsel, but be mindful of legal fees eating into your contract value.

Getting Paid

Make payment easy. Consider using e-payment options like PayPal, despite fees. For instance, a 3% fee on a $10,000 contract might seem high, but it's worth it for quick, hassle-free collection.

Prioritize getting paid upfront for annual contracts. Avoid accounts-receivable headaches by using simple solutions like FreshBooks with e-payment options enabled.

Customer Success Prep

Facilitate a smooth transition to customer success. Schedule kickoff calls or training, and capture relevant information for future use. This includes names, titles, and contact information for decision-makers, executive sponsors, and users.

Close Losting

It's normal not to win every deal. A 20-30% win rate is typical for new solutions. Don't be ashamed of closing deals as lost; it's better than wasting time on dead opportunities.

When to Close Lost

Close lost when objections can't be overcome or when the prospect goes dark. Be direct and give the prospect an offramp. For example, you might send an email like:

> We've missed a couple follow-up appointments. While I think our solution would be valuable to your organization, I don't want to occupy your time if it's unlikely we'll be able to help. Are you still interested in becoming a customer? Is now a bad time? Or does this not make sense for your company after all? I can take the truth, but I'd like clarity.

Don't burn bridges. Remember, your contact might move to another company and want to purchase your solution in their new role.

Closed Lost Metadata

Document reasons for lost deals in your CRM. This helps with future resurrections and informs your product roadmap. Include:

- A picklist of competitors if you lost to competition
- A text field for closed lost notes
- Specific reasons why the deal didn't close

Think of this as creating a treasure map for your future self when you revisit the opportunity.

Coming Back Around

Don't do "one and done" engagements. Circle back after a set time, typically 60 days if no specific timeline was given. For example:

> *Hey Jim! We spoke a few months ago about how TalentBin can help accelerate your technical recruiting, but it wasn't the right time. We've shipped new features, and I see you're still hiring engineers. Want to catch up on what's new in your world and the new hotness we've made?*

Consider prospects targets until they stop having the need you solve or implement a competitor's solution. Regularly revisit closed lost opportunities, creating new ones in your CRM. A fresh pass through the funnel can significantly improve close rates.

Remember, you've invested time in discovery and demos, gathering information your competition doesn't have. Harvest that investment by following up consistently. You'll be amazed at how often a renewed approach, showcasing new features and implying future improvements, can turn a previously lost deal into a win.

PIPELINE MANAGEMENT

Managing multiple concurrent deals is a significant adjustment for new sales founders. Depending on your deal cycle and average contract value, you might be juggling dozens of deals simultaneously, each spanning 30 to 180 days.

Staging

Define clear deal stages to track progress. At TalentBin, we used stages like:

1. "Demo Scheduled": Created when an SDR scheduled a demo with a qualified account.
2. "Qualified": After the demo, with an indeterminate next step.
3. "Seeking Approval": Pain validated, but another stakeholder's permission needed.
4. "Sent Proposal": Prospect requested pricing options.
5. "Negotiation": All hurdles passed except price agreement.
6. "Verbal Agreement": Pricing agreed, contract to be sent.
7. "Contract Sent": Waiting for signature.
8. "Closed Won": Contract signed.
9. "Closed Lost": Sale not happening this time.
10. "Closed-Unqualified": Account never had the need for our solution.

Always have explicit next steps for each opportunity, captured in your CRM and calendared. This prevents deals from going sideways due to lack of follow-up.

Cadencing

Set a recurring time for pipeline review. At TalentBin, we had a two-hour team review every Wednesday afternoon. As you grow, you'll understand your "carrying load"—the number of opportunities you can support before dropping balls.

Block time for pipeline execution. You might decide to do three net-new demos a day, leaving time for down-funnel follow-ups. Or have a floating hour daily for pipeline execution. The key is to allocate time, or the work won't get done.

Pipeline Prioritization and Cleaning

Work "close to the money" first. Focus on deals nearest to closing, prioritizing by deal size and ease of closing. For instance, prioritize a $30k deal over a $10k deal if they require similar effort.

Move up your funnel, ensuring all opportunities have calendared next actions. Be ruthless in cleaning out stuck opportunities to make room for new, promising deals.

Use reporting to rank opportunities by stage and projected revenue. Set up checks for:

- Down-funnel opps without activity in 7 days
- Opps stuck in a stage for over two weeks
- Opps without future meetings ("uncovered opps")

Calendar Management and Role Specialization

Segment your work into different "roles" and allocate time accordingly:

- Block 2 hours for prospecting
- 2 hours for initial outreach
- 2 hours for prospect follow-ups
- Time for demos, follow-up meetings, and closing calls
- Time for pipeline cleaning and follow-ups on in-flight opportunities

Consider time-of-day effectiveness:

- Mornings for prospecting and initial outreach
- Midday and early afternoon for calls and demos
- End of day for summary, wrap-up, and email follow-ups

As you grow, consider role specialization. Hiring a Sales Development Rep (SDR) to handle prospecting and appointment setting can significantly increase your efficiency. For example:

- A $50k SDR plus a $120k Account Executive might drive $650k in revenue annually, a 26% cost of sales.
- With a 1:2 SDR to AE ratio, you could see $1.3M annual revenue from $290k salary expense, a 22% cost of sales.
- Compare this to a full-cycle rep at $100k driving $325k annually, a 30% cost of sales.

This specialization not only makes you more efficient but also builds a talent pipeline for future Account Executives. Consider getting an SDR wingman as soon as you can reliably set appointments for yourself.

Remember, managing multiple opportunities is challenging, but being intentional about your down-funnel cadence will position you to close a good chunk of deals. Once closed, your next challenge is customer success—a crucial aspect of SaaS businesses that we'll cover in the next chapter.

CHAPTER 9

Customer Success Basics: Implementation, Ongoing Success & Renewals

In the SaaS world, closing a deal is just the beginning. Customer success is crucial for renewals, upsells, and positive word-of-mouth. Neglecting it can lead to lost revenue and missed opportunities.

WHY CUSTOMER SUCCESS MATTERS

Successful customers are more likely to:

- Renew contracts
- Increase their usage (and spend)
- Provide testimonials and referrals
- Become advocates at industry events

Poor customer success can lead to churn, which significantly impacts revenue growth. For example, with 5% monthly churn, a company could have less than half the revenue it would have with 0% churn after 58 months. Conversely, with 2.5% monthly expansion, revenue could exceed $7 million MRR in the same period.

Customer success is even more critical when starting out. Early adopters' success makes it easier to win subsequent customers who will take less of a leap of faith.

WHAT IS GOOD CUSTOMER SUCCESS?

It's about fulfilling the promises made during the sales process. Deliver on the KPIs and value propositions outlined in your Sales Narrative for all stakeholders involved. For example:

- TalentBin: Drive more engineering talent into the customer's hiring funnel
- Textio: Optimize job postings for more and diverse applicants

Approach customer success methodically and in stages, similar to your sales pipeline management.

Implementation

Implementation is the first step towards customer success. It includes:

1. Technical setup (credentials, integrations, data migration)
2. User training for all relevant roles
3. Setting expectations and timelines

Tailor your implementation process to your product's complexity. It could be a 30-minute call or a multi-month engagement. Ensure your pricing supports the required level of customer success. For instance, Textio's implementation might include:

- Securing credentials for all recruiters
- Training sessions for users and management
- Integration with the customer's applicant tracking system

Consider charging an implementation fee for resource-intensive setups. A good rule of thumb is to triple the associated labor costs.

Implementation Calls

For straightforward solutions, a 60-minute call can suffice. Include:

1. Pre-call planning:
   - Review CRM notes about users, decision-makers, and purchase rationale

- Prepare necessary materials and complete pre-work (e.g., loading client logo)
- Research the client's business and specific users

2. Rediscovery:
    - Confirm the customer's goals and use cases
    - Example: "You're hiring a dozen software engineers this year, mix of Ruby and front-end. Is that correct?"
    - Document agreed-upon goals in your CRM or follow-up email

3. Agenda items:
    - Critical setup (logins, software installation, data feeds)
    - Core product actions
    - Hands-on practice

Prioritize agenda items from crucial to optional. Ensure basics like login access and necessary software installation are covered first.

Have users actively participate by sharing their screen and performing real tasks. This ensures engagement and immediate value realization. Use tools like Zoom.us or GoToMeeting for screen sharing and remote control. For example, a TalentBin implementation call might include:

- Setting up a job requisition project folder
- Creating and saving a search
- Demonstrating profile viewing and dismissal
- Reaching out to viable candidates
- Setting up drip-recruiting marketing campaigns

By the end of the call, the user should have completed actual work that contributes to ROI.

Remember, your implementation process should align with your demo script, showcasing the most important elements of your solution in a logical, progressive fashion. It's like a demo where the user is in the driver's seat.

IMPLEMENTATION STRATEGIES

Group Calls vs. One-on-Ones

Avoid group implementation calls. They lack accountability and can create "churn time bombs." Everyone thinks someone else is responsible for paying attention, resulting in half-trained, half-implemented users.

Prioritize one-on-one sessions, especially early in your go-to-market. If each user represents $1k of revenue (multiplied by years of renewals), don't skimp on individual attention.

Push back against managers who request group trainings. Explain that while it's an hour per user either way, separate calls provide more value and drive success.

Follow-Up and Monitoring

- Set a back-check meeting for a couple weeks out.
- Assign specific, measurable homework. For example, Teamable might assign reaching out to 100 referral candidates (10 from 10 internal staff) in the first week.
- Use SaaS monitoring to track user actions. Make it clear you'll be watching to ensure success and report ROI to deal sponsors.
- Schedule follow-up meetings before ending implementation calls to avoid chasing customers later.

Emphasize that users who complete homework have X% more success, justifying the assignment.

Materials and Support

Provide easy access to support, recorded onboarding calls, and implementation scripts. If possible, record individual onboarding calls for future reference.

Consider weekly "group implementations" for refreshers or new users to balance efficiency and effectiveness.

Multistage Implementations

For complex solutions:

1. Treat it like a multistage sales process.
2. Hold a kickoff call with all stakeholders. Restate the customer's goal and walk through necessary steps and timelines.
3. Use visual aids like timeline slides or shared Google Sheets for project tracking.
4. Provide regular status updates.

Example project tracking spreadsheet:

- Create a templated Google Sheet with columns for deliverables/actions, customer-side owners, target dates, and status.
- Identify stakeholders for each item (e.g., "CMO owns this, VP of IT owns that").
- Use this as a "source of truth" throughout the implementation process.

Advanced Progress Tracking

Move from spreadsheets to CRM tracking for better querying across multiple implementations. Options include:

- A post-sales status field on opportunities correlated with implementation stages.
- Distinct activity items associated with closed opportunities.

This allows queries like, "Show all opportunities closed in the last 14 days without an initial kickoff call."

Implementation Execution

Be proactive in completing tasks for customers when possible. Example: Outreach.io's approach to Salesforce integration:

- Schedule a specific call with the customer's Salesforce admin.
- Use screen-sharing software to take control (with permission) and complete the setup.

Handling Snags

1. Reschedule missed meetings promptly.
2. Communicate implications of delays to stakeholders. For example: "We need this 15-minute call to complete XYZ, which is required for the next step that [stakeholder name] wants done by [date]."
3. Document all efforts in emails, meeting invites, and status updates in case of future issues.
4. Be cautious about escalating to sponsors for uncooperative stakeholders to avoid potential negative repercussions.

Completion and Charging

1. Memorialize completion to deal sponsors, signaling it's time to expect ROI.
2. Consider charging for complex implementations as a professional service, especially if they vary significantly between customers. For example, if a customer needs integration with 3-4 systems requiring 20+ hours from your team, you might charge extra for that service.

Remember, the goal is to ensure customer success and prevent churn. Tailor your approach based on your product's complexity and pricing model. Good implementation can be a competitive advantage, making it harder for customers to switch away from your solution.

CUSTOMER SUCCESS CALENDAR MANAGEMENT & SPECIALIZATION

Inducements for Users/Stakeholders

Provide incentives for users to embrace implementation:

- Emphasize how the solution enhances their professional development
- Offer certification programs (e.g., TalentBin Certification)
    1. Include digital PDF certificates and an employer-checkable registry
    2. Align certification with actions that drive ROI for their companies

- Send company schwag (e.g., T-shirts, Post-it notes, high-quality pens). Even $5 worth of items can make a big difference for a $1000/year user.

Compensate customer success staff based on success precursor metrics (e.g., proportion of users logged in last 30 days) or customer satisfaction scores, rather than renewal metrics.

INBOUND RESPONSE & SUPPORT TICKETS

Inbound Support Request Capture

- Ensure low friction for contacting support
- Use a prominent "Help" or "Support" link
- Options include:
  1. Simple mailto: link to support@yourdomain.com
  2. Google Form for structured information (be cautious of added friction)
  3. Shared-inbox solutions (e.g., Front, Help Scout)
  4. Ticketing systems (e.g., Zendesk, Desk.com, Freshdesk, Salesforce ServiceCloud)

General Support Tenets

- Focus on diffusing frustration first
- Take responsibility for issues, avoid blaming the user
- Validate the source of frustration
- Persist until the problem is resolved or the user confirms it's no longer an issue

Rapid Response

- Aim for quick response times, even if it's just acknowledging the ticket
- Consider direct phone calls for rapid problem-solving in early stages
- Communicate expected follow-up time frames

Response Tracking

- Use support software to track ticket status (new, in progress, done)
- Practice good hygiene when responding to requests
- Get affirmative statements that issues are resolved before closing tickets

Canned Responses and Macros

- Create templates for common issues to improve efficiency
- Develop support articles for frequently asked questions
- Use macros in support software to quickly deploy responses and update ticket statuses

Ticket Tagging/Product Feedback

- Tag tickets to identify patterns and guide product development
- Example: Textio might tag editor-related issues with "editor" and "saving"
- Use tagging to inform monthly product development decisions

OTHER INBOUND SUPPORT TOOLS

Live Chat

- Provides immediacy and easier information gathering
- Allows support agents to handle multiple conversations simultaneously
- Consider tools like Intercom or Zendesk Chat, which can switch between chat and email modes

Social Support

- Monitor social media (especially Twitter) for customer issues
- Treat social comments as initial support requests
- Acknowledge publicly, then move to private channels for resolution
- Use social listening tools as you grow
- Leverage social media for positive interactions and sales opportunities

Phone Support

- Consider offering phone support early on for white-glove treatment
- Use phone interactions to gather valuable customer insights
- Be prepared to adjust or remove this option as you scale

Remember, the goal is to ensure customers achieve the value promised during the sales process. Good support can often compensate for early product issues. Prioritize customer success to drive renewals, upsells, and positive word-of-mouth. As you grow, continually evaluate and adjust your support strategies to balance customer satisfaction with operational efficiency.

PROACTIVE CUSTOMER SUCCESS STRATEGIES

Proactive Customer Monitoring

SaaS delivery allows us to monitor customer usage, crucial for preventing churn. Implement:

1. Inspection: Log in as users to check for proper usage. This helps troubleshoot and verify value precursors.

2. Custom Reporting: Develop reports on key value precursors and outcomes. Two types:

    - Comprehensive reports for trailing time intervals
    - Prescriptive reports alerting you to users below usage thresholds

3. Dedicated Tooling: Use tools like Mixpanel for basic tracking, or Gainsight/Catalyst for advanced customer success instrumentation.

Act on this data by reviewing regularly and addressing issues proactively. Approach users from a helpful standpoint, reminding them of the value props. Common issues include:

- Competing time demands (help with prioritization)
- Feature confusion (provide guidance)
- User turnover (re-implement with new users)
- Resistant users (make your case or involve deal sponsors)

Focus efforts on "C+/B-" users to elevate them to "B+" levels, rather than trying to save "F" and "D" users or spending time on already successful "A" users.

Success Outcome Capture

Document customer success for renewals and marketing materials:

1. In-product capture: Design features to track success metrics (e.g., TalentBin's "hired" stage for candidates).
    - Capture both direct outcomes and precursors (e.g., Textio tracking improved job posting scores and application ratios)
2. Surveys/Conversations: Use tools like AskNicely or Delighted for regular feedback.
    - Implement at set intervals (e.g., 45 days post-kickoff) or embed in UI
    - Include standard NPS questions and specific value capture queries

Store this data in your CRM for easy reporting on customer success timelines. This allows you to answer questions like:

- How quickly do customers reach ROI payback?
- What proportion of customers achieve success in the first, second, or third month?

Quarterly Business Reviews (QBRs)

Use QBRs to reflect success back to customers, reminding them of the value they're getting. Benefits include:

- Keeping your solution top-of-mind

- Facilitating upsells and word-of-mouth promotion
- Reinforcing commitment bias against competitors

QBR components:

1. Participants: Include decision-makers and key stakeholders. Focus on primary decision-makers if user base is too large.
2. Content: Use a slide deck template covering:
   - Shared goals and rediscovery (e.g., "You purchased TalentBin to hire Ruby on Rails engineers. Is this still your priority?")
   - KPI improvements (before and after implementation)
   - Adoption rates and ROI (highlight opportunity costs of non-adoption)
   - Issues and proposed solutions (address known problems proactively)
   - Next steps and recommendations (e.g., retraining, upsells, or marketing participation)
3. Delivery:
   - On-site for larger customers (can include user training or appreciation events)
   - Digital presentations for others (record for future reference)
   - Consider automated QBRs for low-cost solutions
4. Follow-up:
   - Summarize action items in an email
   - Start execution immediately, as the clock is ticking until the next QBR
5. Reporting:
   - Track QBR execution in your CRM
   - Set up "QBR" events with completion states ("To Be Scheduled," "Scheduled," "Completed")

- Automate quarterly intervals for scheduling when deals close
- Run reports to see upcoming QBRs needing scheduling and preparation

Remember, proactive customer success is about identifying and addressing issues early, documenting wins, and consistently demonstrating value to your customers. This approach drives renewals, upsells, and positive word-of-mouth. By implementing these strategies, you're not just reacting to problems, but actively ensuring your customers achieve the promised ROI and remain loyal to your solution.

CUSTOMER SUCCESS MATERIALS AND RENEWALS

Support Sites & Asynchronous Support Materials

Create a support site with how-to articles, videos, and FAQs. Benefits include:

- Consistent, accurate information
- Self-service problem-solving for customers
- Freeing up success staff for complex issues

Start with basics like recorded kickoff calls, then expand based on common questions. Break down implementation videos into topic-specific snippets for easier reference.

Use support software analytics to understand usage and identify areas for improvement. Create new articles when questions come up more than once.

When using support notes to answer queries:

1. Explain why you think the note will help
2. Offer to discuss further if needed
3. Avoid appearing to "stiff-arm" customers who prefer human interaction

New Release Communications

Regularly update customers on new features to:

- Address known pain points

- Demonstrate ongoing product improvement
- Reengage at-risk customers

Create materials like:

1. Support site notes explaining feature goals and usage
2. Demo videos or animated GIFs
3. Email announcements
4. In-product banners or fly-ins

Share with both users and decision-makers to maintain engagement and uncover upsell opportunities. Add stakeholders to your CRM for targeted communications.

Implement and monitor adoption of new features, providing additional training as needed. Example: TalentBin's "automated follow-up campaigns" feature required customization, so the team scheduled implementation calls with existing customers.

Renewals

The goal of customer success is to ensure renewals. Strategies include:

1. Automatic renewals:
   - Include in contracts with courtesy emails before renewal date
   - Helps with delayed implementations or stakeholder turnover
   - Can lock in favorable pricing for customers
2. Renewal calls: Similar to QBRs, summarize success over the entire term.
   - Time 6-8 weeks before contract end
   - Schedule after the final QBR
   - Prepare with comprehensive success metrics from CRM
   - Discuss business goals for the upcoming year
   - Create a "grand finale" QBR deck with all success metrics

3. Timing and preparation:
   - Start addressing potential issues at the second-to-last QBR
   - Consider short-term contract extensions to resolve last-minute problems
4. Closing and upselling:
   - Always ask for the business, even with auto-renewals
   - Validate customer buy-in: "Your contract will be renewing on [date]. We're looking forward to working together in the year ahead."
   - Use discussions about future goals to uncover upsell opportunities. Example: If a customer plans to hire 30 new salespeople, propose buying additional seats now for a volume discount

Remember, the key to renewals is ensuring customers get value throughout their contract term. By focusing on ongoing success, clear communication, and proactive problem-solving, you set the stage for smooth renewals and potential growth. Consistently demonstrate the ROI of your solution to make renewal a no-brainer for your customers.

CUSTOMER SUCCESS TEAM MANAGEMENT AND LEARNING

Customer Success can provide valuable insights to other departments:

1. Product Development: Identify challenging features and prioritize improvements.
2. Sales: Alert about user transitions to new companies and provide customer references.
3. Marketing & PR: Supply real-world success stories and data for collateral.
4. Events/Customer Advisory: Identify advocates for conferences and product feedback.

Incentivize the CS team to share this information, e.g., offering bonuses for identifying up-sell opportunities.

CUSTOMER SUCCESS CALENDAR MANAGEMENT & SPECIALIZATION

As responsibilities grow:

1. Schedule CS activities (implementations, QBRs) immediately after deal closure.
2. Track CS activities in CRM for easy reporting.
3. Create a CS playbook after onboarding initial customers.

RESPONSIBILITY SPECIALIZATION & COMPENSATION

Consider CS importance when determining compensation. Two main approaches:

1. CS staff responsible for renewals and upsells, with variable compensation.
2. Split responsibilities: CS for support and Account Managers for renewals/upsells.

Early-stage recommendation: Have CS handle implementation, support, QBRs, and renewals for efficiency.

LATER SPECIALIZATION

As customer base grows, consider specializing roles:

- Inbound support
- Implementation
- Ongoing success management
- Account management and renewals

This allows for efficiency and scaled service levels.

Remember, the most critical factor is prioritizing customer success from the start. Having a success mindset and choosing appropriate approaches will put you ahead of many competitors.

CHAPTER 10

Early Sales Management & Scaling Concepts

What the hell is "scaling?" In B2B sales organizations, it's when you take something proven to work at the unit level—one sales rep or "pod"—and start adding more to parallelize your go-to-market. Most B2B organizations scale revenue acquisition not by magically selling more through existing reps, but by adding more reps. Your job shifts from creating the "way to sell this" to building an organization that implements that approach repeatedly and scalably.

SCALING ANTI-PATTERNS & KNOWING WHEN TO HIT THE GAS

Premature Scaling

This involves adding sales staff before proving the sales motion works. It typically results in an inefficient go-to-market effort that burns cash, destroys enterprise value, and often leads to layoffs. A common scenario is a founder hiring a sales leader and team before personally validating the sales process. This can lead to inefficient reps, customer satisfaction problems, and selling to unsuitable prospects just to close deals.

Lagged Scaling

This is when a founder or early salesperson gets stuck "turning the crank" on more deals instead of moving to the next challenge. While less common and less existentially threatening than premature scaling, it's problematic in its own way. It's about eating opportunity cost—the longer you wait to "package" your sales ability for others, the more time you lose to competitors and the slower you build enterprise value.

When is the Right Time to Scale?

It's not a binary situation, but more like easing into a hot jacuzzi, validating as you go. Key indicators include:

1. A consistent win rate between 15-30%. If you're reliably in this range, it's time to bring on other reps and prove you can get them to close at a similar pace.
2. Cost of sales at 20-25% of revenue. Your AE, SDR, and sales engineer costs should not exceed 25% of the revenue they close.
3. Reliable average contract value and deal cycle.

For example, if a rep doing 5 new demos a week with a 20% win rate and $10k average deal value can bring in $480k a year, that's efficient. But at a 10% win rate, they'd only bring in $240k—potentially making the cost of sales too high.

Remember, having a good win rate, coupled with a solid average contract value and consistent deal cycle, is a good leading indicator of readiness to scale. Otherwise, you'll be hitting the accelerator on a car that leaks most of the gas out of the engine.

ABSTRACTION & SPECIALIZATION OF SALES ROLES

As we scale up, we need to prove that AEs other than you can successfully sell the solution, and that CS staff can successfully implement and drive customer success. This prepares you for hiring and managing many of these roles, allowing you to ramp up your organization's revenue.

Role Specialization

Specialization of sales and success staff is a powerful "modern" way of selling. The benefits include:

1. Individuals become better at their specialized tasks

2. Reduced context switching costs
3. Enabled by CRM as a central repository of truth

The gold standard is a specialized setup with SDRs setting appointments, AEs pitching and running deals, and CSM/AMs "farming" accounts. However, specialization might not be necessary for low-price, transactional deals.

Specialization and Sales Maturity Stages

We approach scale-out in stages, validating hypotheses along the way:

1. **Founder Doing It All:** Prove you can convince customers of your solution's value and get them to pay for it.
2. **Founder Plus SDR / Founder Plus CSM:** Add either an SDR for lead generation or a CSM for customer support, depending on your needs.
3. **Founder Plus SDR and Two AEs:** Prove that non-founder sellers can sell the solution. Focus on hiring, training, and management.
4. **Initial "Sales Pod":** Founder steps out of day-to-day selling. Prove successful performance of a complete revenue production unit.
5. **"Sales Pod" Abstraction & Initial Scale:** Clone the initial sales pod to double or triple throughput. Focus on metrics and analytics.
6. **Full Scaled Sales Team of Teams:** Hand off to professional sales managers to continue scaling.

Sales Operations

Sales operations focuses on making the entire sales "machine" more fluid and effective through metrics analysis, process refinement, and technology adoption. It typically makes sense to introduce a dedicated sales ops role when you have enough reps (around 10) to justify the cost.

Even before that, sales ops responsibilities fall on you as the leader, other managers, and the reps themselves. Think of it as the "product management of the sales org," constantly looking to enhance the go-to-market by removing friction and adding functionality.

EARLY SALES MANAGEMENT

Sales management is the practice of enabling, coaching, inspecting, correcting, and managing groups of salespeople to take your product to market. Success is driven by a high quantity of high-quality customer-facing selling activity. We can improve output by raising either the quantity of sales activity, the quality, or both.

THE ROLE OF THE SALES MANAGER

As a sales manager, your mindset must shift from "doing" sales to helping others do the selling. Your job is to achieve scale through successful hiring, onboarding, training, monitoring, and coaching of reps. Remember, adding more efficient reps is more valuable than your individual sales performance.

For example, if you close 30% of first demos at a $50k average deal size, while your reps close at 20% for $30k, you might think you should keep selling. Wrong. Your $80k per month is nothing compared to adding four reps each bringing in $50k. Your goal is to figure out how to make your reps perform at your level.

Manager Activities

1. Hiring & Onboarding:
   - Approach hiring with the same rigor as your selling activities.
   - Implement intense, detailed onboarding to get reps off to a successful start.
   - Filter out the wrong people during hiring, not after they've started.
2. Process Construction and Monitoring:
   - Formalize and document your sales process, including qualification criteria and handoff points.
   - Monitor execution, verify adherence, and refine as needed.
   - Select and administer tools that act as force multipliers for your process.

3. Metrics Harness Construction & Monitoring:
   - Build and monitor a performance metrics system to track rep activities and results.
   - Use this as an early warning system for issues with individual reps or market shifts.
   - Let metrics guide your coaching and process refinement efforts.
4. Inspection, Coaching, and Correction:
   - Regularly inspect rep activities, identify improvement areas, and correct underlying issues.
   - Don't shy away from giving direct feedback. Your willingness to correct is crucial for the team's success.
   - Use metrics to guide these conversations and make them data-driven.
5. Materials & Documentation:
   - Create and maintain documentation for onboarding and ongoing rep support.
   - This includes objection handling guides, call recordings, and updated sales decks.
   - Prioritize this "administrative" work—it's a key point of leverage for your entire team.
6. Performance Management & Professional Development:
   - Focus on identifying growth opportunities for staff and addressing performance issues.
   - Implement regular one-on-ones and performance reviews.
   - Help reps progress in their careers to reduce churn.
   - Monitor employee engagement and morale, not just performance metrics.

Remember, these activities are different from individual selling. Your job is to spread your validated, repeatable selling motion across a growing number of reps. You're no longer a player, but a coach; no longer a doer, but a teacher.

By focusing on these management activities, you'll set your sales organization on the path to scalable growth and success. When you eventually move to managing other managers, knowing these activities cold will help you monitor whether they're happening sufficiently within your managerial base.

The Modern Metrical Sales Manager

In modern sales organizations, managers use metrics to continuously monitor the quantity and quality of reps' selling activities. This approach allows managers to focus their time on addressing specific improvement areas, rather than being overwhelmed with all rep activities.

To implement this approach:

1. Goal Setting: Define clear, measurable goals for your team and individual roles. For example, $80k of new business bookings per month per rep, or 10 new qualified meetings per SDR per week.

2. Sales Methods Definition & Benchmark Setting: Document your sales process and set baseline metrics for each activity. This should be based on your founding selling experience. Define the number of meetings, types of meetings, customer-facing calls and emails, unique accounts engaged, and opportunities worked. Set quantitative benchmarks for each.

3. Recording & Capturing Selling Activity: Implement systems (like CRMs) to record all relevant sales activities. This goes beyond just deals closed and revenue booked. Record customer-facing meetings, different types of meetings, emails, calls, presentations, and proposals. Automation can help here, like using Zoom and Chorus to record digital presentations.

4. Metrics Consumption: Regularly review metrics in your operational cadence. Set recurring calendar events for yourself to review metrics. Include a "metrics section" in team meetings, review individual metrics in one-on-ones, and have a metrics section in monthly post-mortems.

5. Anomaly Detection: Look for concerning divergences from goals or team averages. For instance, if a rep's win rate drops from 25% to 15% over two months while others maintain 25%, that's concerning. Positive anomalies are worth investigating too.

6. Root Causing Issues: Dig deeper into metrics to find the underlying causes of performance issues. Think of metrics as a tree—if bookings are down, is it fewer deals or smaller deal sizes? If fewer deals, is it a lower win rate or fewer opportunities? Keep digging until you find the root cause.

7. Sales Motion Inspection: When metrics aren't enough, inspect actual calls, meetings, and emails. Use tools like Chorus or Gong to listen to recorded calls, or ride along on new deals. For SDRs with lagging metrics, you might need to review their actual email content.

8. Coaching & Spreading Success: Address identified issues through specific coaching and practice. Demonstrate the correct way to execute a selling activity, then engage in mock repetitions until the rep gets it right. When you identify best practices, capture and spread them to the rest of the team.

Remember, this isn't micromanagement—it's effective management. Think of it like a sports coach analyzing player performance and practicing to improve. Can you imagine a scenario where a professional baseball player has an identified performance issue, and the coach was afraid to help him resolve it because it felt like "micromanagement"? The concept sounds absurd. Sales management is no different.

By using metrics to guide your management, you can make your sales organization more efficient. You might only need one $200k sales manager for every 8 reps instead of every 5, reducing management overhead by 40% and improving your cost of sales and valuations.

Even with great onboarding, issues will crop up. Your job as a manager is to identify these issues early through metrics, diagnose the root causes, and implement solutions to keep your team performing at its best. And when you spot high performers, use the same process to identify what they're doing right and spread those practices across the team.

Stage-Specific Management Rigor and Sales Performance Instrumentation

Early On

With your first couple of reps, it's fine to over-invest time in monitoring and inspection. Sit in on calls and be CC'd on prospect communication to understand how deals are progressing. This helps you learn common issues in your sales motion, allowing you to iterate your onboarding and training for future cohorts.

At Scale

As you grow to six reps or more, implement a solid metrics harness to identify early warning indicators and "zoom in" on potential hot spots. This approach will benefit your organization and help future sales managers ensure good yields on hiring classes and quicker identification of issues.

Sales Performance Instrumentation

Successful sales behavior comes from a high quantity of high-quality customer-facing selling activity. Instrument both inputs and outputs—don't fall into the trap of only caring about outputs.

Quantity, Quality, and Mix

1. Quantity Metrics: Counts of activities like customer meetings, emails sent, calls made, opportunities created, deals won/lost, revenue booked, etc.
2. Quality Metrics: Ratios and averages like win rate, average deal size, pipeline conversion rate, etc.

Different roles may focus on different metrics. For example, SDRs might focus more on activity metrics like meetings created and pipeline generated.

Quality metrics can also be used for reporting on deals with less-than-stellar execution, like untouched opportunities.

Reading Metrics

A great metrics harness provides a behavioral fingerprint for each sales rep, allowing you to:

1. Understand the behaviors of your best reps
2. See changes in rep performance over time
3. Monitor new hire ramp-up
4. Identify potential issues with rep motivation before they become major problems

At TalentBin, we tracked bookings, demo meetings, proposals sent, and email activity for AEs. For quality metrics, we monitored win rate, average deal size, deal cycle, and untouched opportunities. For SDRs, we tracked demo creation, email and calling quantity, unique accounts engaged, calling connect rates, and win rate on opportunities created.

Remember, it's okay to start basic and get more advanced later. The important thing is to start instrumenting your sales process so you're not flying blind.

Managerial Operational Cadence

To ensure important tasks get done, implement "operational cadences" or "operational rhythms." Chop your workdays, weeks, and months into manageable time blocks with specific checkpoints and recurring activities.

On Meetings

Meetings, when done correctly, ensure that necessary tasks get done. They are for rich communication, ensuring organizational alignment, and addressing issues proactively. Without them, core needs will still exist but will be served in less effective ways, potentially eroding morale or leading to misaligned priorities.

How to Implement Operational Cadence Meetings

- Have a stated purpose, attendees, format, length, and cadence
- Use calendar invites with recurring time frames and specific agendas

- Be efficient with attendees—only include those who are necessary
- Constrain time frames to what's needed—no sprawl
- Pay attention to meeting timing (e.g., during lunch, at day's edges)
- Set explicit content and format to avoid purpose dilution
- Cadence ensures follow-up and accountability

Examples of Sales-centric Operational Cadence Meetings

1. Sales Stand ups
   - Purpose: Daily checkpoint, shared learning, transparent accountability
   - Format: <30 seconds per person on key metrics (demos, calls, emails)
   - Cadence: Daily or twice daily, <10 minutes
   - Anti-purpose: Not for exhaustive rehashing or strategy questioning

2. Sales Team meeting
   - Purpose: Review metrics, promote accountability, share product/CS info
   - Format: Review team metrics, product updates, CS updates, personal wins/learnings
   - Cadence: Weekly, 60 minutes (Mondays, lunch)
   - Attendees: Entire sales team, product leadership rep, CS rep

3. Pipeline meeting
   - Purpose: Shared accountability and focused pipeline maintenance
   - Format: Review closed deals, likely closures, pipeline maintenance
   - Cadence: Weekly, 60-120 minutes (Wednesday end of day)
   - Anti-purpose: Not for ideation or complaining

4. One-on-ones
   - Purpose: Extract issues, share information privately
   - Format: "What do you need from me?", "What do I need from you?", "What do you need to know?"
   - Cadence: Every two weeks, 30-60 minutes
   - Anti-purpose: Not a status or pipeline review
5. Monthly Retrospective
   - Purpose: Review prior month, plan for current month
   - Format: Review goal metrics, diagnose issues, share successes
   - Cadence: Monthly, 60 minutes (beginning of month, over lunch)
   - Attendees: Entire sales team, potentially product leadership and CS rep
6. End of Time Period Celebration
   - Purpose: Drive team camaraderie
   - Format: Team lunch or dinner
   - Cadence: Monthly, after close of prior month
7. Executive Meeting (CEO and Sales Lead)
   - Purpose: Track progress against sales goals
   - Format: Review key metrics, discuss constraints, agree on solutions
   - Cadence: Every two weeks, 30-60 minutes (end of day)
   - Anti-purpose: Not a one-on-one for performance issues
8. Quarterly Business Review
   - Add this on a quarterly basis as a more robust version of the monthly retrospective
   - Focus on clear-eyed evaluation of execution to date and future expectations

Example Operational Cadence Calendar

- Daily: Sales standups
- Weekly: Sales team meeting (Monday), Pipeline meeting (Wednesday)
- Bi-weekly: One-on-ones, Executive meeting
- Monthly: Retrospective, End of period celebration
- Quarterly: Business review

Implement these meetings consistently to ensure your sales organization stays on track and issues are addressed proactively. Remember, the key is to make these meetings purposeful, efficient, and tailored to your team's needs.

Adding Managerial Layers

Add management help when you can no longer handle all tasks effectively. Conventional wisdom suggests issues arise with 6-9 direct reports. This typically occurs somewhere between having an initial "sales pod" and multiple pods.

The better your metrics harness and documentation, the longer you can manage without additional help. However, don't wait too long—your team might be under-performing by 10-30% without dedicated management.

Consider adding team leads as a short-term solution. They can handle metrics monitoring, report outs, and act as a first line of defense for questions. However, people management topics like one-on-ones and hiring typically remain with you.

Eventually, you'll need a full managerial layer. The time is right when you can't handle all responsibilities in a 40-60 hour work week. Remember, your highest leverage activity at this point might be hiring and onboarding rather than day-to-day management.

Professional Development & Promotion Paths

Focusing on professional development is crucial for retention and value creation. For example, successfully promoting an SDR to AE can add $400k in monthly enterprise value. Similarly, developing a mid-market rep to an enterprise AE can add millions in organizational value.

Development paths typically include:

1. Individual contributor progression (e.g., SDR to AE, AE to enterprise AE)
2. Managerial path

For SDRs aiming to become AEs, focus on practicing discovery calls, open-ended questions, presentations, and objection handling. For AEs and CSMs, involve them in larger, more complex deals.

For those on the managerial path, assign projects that make the team more successful or specific management tasks. This could include tooling, process projects, or improving specific parts of your sales motion.

Discuss preferred paths with each team member and tailor their development accordingly. Schedule regular time for these activities, such as a couple of hours weekly.

Building a Strong Organizational Culture

Culture is the set of implicit behaviors your organization considers appropriate or inappropriate. It acts as operational "spackle" filling gaps between management processes. As Netflix put it, company values are shown by who gets rewarded, promoted, or let go.

To foster an intentional culture:

1. Specification: Determine what culture aligns with your markets, recruitment goals, and existing team. Consider:

    - What markets do you sell into? (e.g., conservative like healthcare or informal like dev tools)
    - Who do you want to recruit? (Junior or senior staff?)
    - What's the existing culture from founders and early employees?

2. Documentation: Create a shared document outlining your values and anti-values. It doesn't need to be as extensive as Netflix's culture deck, but should be easily referenceable.

3. Articulation: Proactively share and reinforce your culture from hiring through all aspects of employee experience. Use it in interviews to attract aligned candidates and screen out poor fits. Weave it into onboarding, team meetings, and all-hands gatherings.

A strong culture can be a competitive advantage, supporting execution, attracting talent, and improving retention. Conversely, a misaligned culture can lead to serious issues, as seen with companies like Zenefits where a culture of shortcuts collided with highly regulated markets. Remember, culture isn't set in stone—it can evolve, but it needs to be intentionally shaped and consistently reinforced.

CHAPTER 11

High-Impact Sales Hiring

As your go-to-market strategy proves successful, it's time to scale by adding more people. SaaS sales organizations traditionally grow by incrementally adding humans to execute sales tasks. While challenging due to the complexities of hiring and managing unfamiliar people, getting the right professionals on board can be transformative. High-quality hires create a positive flywheel effect, improving business outcomes and attracting more top talent.

Quality hiring is crucial for early-stage sales organizations ready to scale. In a greenfield market, it's a land grab, and every week without the right staff gives competitors an advantage. Bad hires can be detrimental, costing you missed opportunities and lost customers. The ability to attract and onboard successful sales staff can be a significant competitive edge against incumbents.

As you grow, focus on specialization. Start by hiring market development help to generate leads, then add account executives when your calendar is overloaded. Later, bring in account managers for renewals.

When determining your hiring profile, look for:

1. Raw characteristics:

    - High intellectual acumen

    - Strong "figure shit out quotient" (practical street smarts)

    - High "grinder quotient" (ability to persist through unpleasant tasks)

2. Professional characteristics:
   - Smarts (top-tier education or pattern of achievement)
   - Resourcefulness (history of "figuring things out")
   - Competitiveness (sports or academic competition experience)
   - Coachability (experience taking and implementing feedback)
   - Likability and leadership (positions in teams or organizations)
   - Detail orientation (organized, methodical approach)
   - Persistence (endurance sports, long-term projects)
   - Positivity (ability to handle rejection and setbacks)
   - Teamwork (collaborative experiences)

Look for these traits in candidates to build a strong foundation for your sales team. Remember, the presence of these characteristics doesn't replace proper screening and interviewing but gives you a great starting point for building an effective sales organization.

Professional Characteristics

When hiring more senior staff, consider prior experience carefully. I'm torn between creating an "upwelling" effect by training fresh college graduates and hiring experienced professionals for quick scaling.

Be cautious about:

1. Industry Focus: Look for those who've sold to the same decision-makers at similar price points and budgetary tempos.
2. Role Execution Focus: Ensure the candidate's experience matches your needs (e.g., new customer acquisition vs. renewals).
3. Sales Cycle Tempo: Match candidates' experience with your solution's sales cycle length.
4. Industry Bellwethers: Be wary of reps from established brands who may struggle without those advantages.

Good sources for hires include:

- Mid-stage startups in your space
- Customers familiar with your problem space

Achievement Characteristics

Ask for proof of achievements:

- Screenshots of activity graphs and leaderboards from their CRM
- W2s (though these only show top-line outcomes)

Prefer data from third-party sources over resumes or LinkedIn profiles.

Relationships or "Hiring a Rolodex"

The concept of hiring for a salesperson's relationships is outdated. With tools like LinkedIn and Data.com, identifying decision-makers is easier than ever. Don't compromise on other criteria just to access someone's contacts.

Remember, a young market development rep with the right tools can often achieve the same results as an experienced hire with an outdated rolodex.

Articulating and Documenting Your Hiring Profile

Consider how successful SaaS sales organizations approach their hiring profiles:

1. TalentBin: We targeted new grads from top universities (Stanford, Cal, other UC schools) with a history of achievement, initiative, and team/athletic excellence. We also hired market development staff from LinkedIn, offering faster paths to account executive roles. Former technical recruiters with high subject-matter expertise and execution skills were also valuable. We avoided senior staff from legacy organizations who were used to selling established solutions.

2. Meraki: They successfully pulled staff from IT value-added reseller (VAR) shops. These professionals had to hustle hard in undifferentiated markets, often served in consultative roles, and were adept at understanding customer pain and matching new technologies to solve problems.

3. Yelp/Groupon: With low average contract values and a massive market, they focused on recent grads from regional colleges (e.g., Arizona State, San Francisco State) for high-volume, transactional sales. They sought charismatic, articulate, non-technical staff to handle thousands of smaller contracts.

Document your hiring profile in an easily shareable format, like a Google Doc with public viewing access.

SOURCES OF HIRE

Staffing Agencies

- Excellent for first hires, providing ready-to-go, qualified candidates
- Typically charge 20-30% of first-year salary
- Target sales-specific agencies (e.g., TheLions, Betts Recruiting, Rainmakers)
- Be clear about your desired profile to avoid mismatches
- Screen candidates thoroughly, despite pre-vetting
- Consider the "network value" of early hires from agencies
- Limit to 1-2 agencies to avoid overwhelm
- Use the "one in, one out" rule to ensure quality candidates

Referral Recruiting

- Highest-quality, lowest-cost source once established
- Provide staff with easily shareable job descriptions and hiring profiles
- Offer referral bonuses ($2,500-$5,000) to incentivize staff
- Regularly remind your staff of open roles in team meetings
- Proactively review your staff's networks (LinkedIn, Facebook) for potential candidates

- Celebrate successful referral hires to encourage participation
- Provide feedback on referrals to help your staff improve their recommendations

Job Boards

- Can provide high-velocity candidate flow of active job seekers
- Be mindful of increased screening needs
- Clearly state requirements and "nice-to-haves" in job postings
- Consider mentioning your screening process to attract motivated candidates
- Aim for about a dozen quality resumes per week
- Adjust posting details based on quantity and quality of applicants

Direct Sourcing

- Search candidate databases like LinkedIn or TalentBin
- Labor-intensive but allows precise targeting of desired profiles
- Particularly effective for sales roles, as they often have detailed LinkedIn profiles
- Use specific search queries to filter candidates (e.g., "SDR" OR "BDR" AND "LinkedIn" OR "Salesforce")
- Contact via email/phone when possible for higher response rates
- Use a "sell, screen, sell" approach for passive candidates
- Don't skip the screening process, even for seemingly qualified candidates

Remember, regardless of source, always maintain a rigorous screening process to ensure quality hires. Bad hires can be extremely costly in terms of missed opportunities and lost customers.

SCREENING, INTERVIEWING, AND CLOSING A NEW HIRE

The screening and interviewing process exists to authenticate that candidates have the characteristics required for success in your sales org. It's about proving their abilities, not just relying on impressive resumes or pedigrees.

Screening

"Artifact-Based" Pre-Screens

I'm a fan of asynchronous screening approaches, like written screens. These put the time cost on the candidate and create rich "interviewing artifacts." Here's what I look for:

1. Clear communication skills
2. Attention to detail
3. Ability to follow instructions
4. Critical thinking

I use a series of open-ended questions, giving candidates an hour to respond. Some examples:

- Tell me about something you've built that you're proud of.
- What do you think about Google Glass?
- Document a deal that went terribly. Be honest.

I also like to include a mini homework assignment, such as leaving a 30-second voicemail pitch for a specific company. This tests initiative, comprehension, and execution levels.

Phone Screen

Use this to authenticate more nuanced parts of the profile. I focus on:

1. Intellectual acumen
2. Problem-solving skills
3. Ability to think on their feet

I ask candidates to walk me through a sales funnel they're familiar with, then dive into questions about optimization, scalability, and problem-solving.

Mock Presentation Screening

For closing roles, I have candidates sell me their existing solution in a full-blown 30-60 minute presentation. I evaluate:

1. Pre-call preparation
2. Discovery process
3. Tailoring of problem and solution statements
4. Handling of objections and questions
5. Closing skills

This is also a great opportunity to test coachability by providing feedback mid-presentation. Remember, maintain a rigorous screening process regardless of a candidate's seniority or pedigree. It's crucial for building a high-quality sales team.

Interviewing

After rigorous screening, on-site team interviews serve to:

1. Catch any missed red flags
2. Get team perspectives
3. Build consensus

Assign specific interview focuses to team members (e.g., recruiting acumen, technology understanding, cultural fit). Provide scripted questions and a unified method for recording outcomes (green/yellow/red flags, summation). I recommend a final "beer interview" with the broader team to:

- Assess cultural fit efficiently
- Allow candid Q&A
- Leverage team quality as a selling point

Document all feedback in the standard format.

Deciding Between Multiple Candidates

In early-stage environments, it's better to have extra salespeople than uncalled accounts. If candidates meet your bar, consider hiring them all—more rainmakers are good.

Reference Checking

1. Provided references:
   - Ask, "On a scale of 1-10, how highly would you recommend the candidate?"
   - Follow up with, "What would they need to do to become a 10?"
2. Back channel references:
   - Find shared connections on LinkedIn/Facebook
   - Look for patterns across multiple references
   - Validate key projects or wins mentioned by the candidate

Post-Interview

Move quickly post-interview. High-quality candidates won't be available long. Momentum is crucial in hiring, just like in sales deals.

If you're unsure, pass. "If there's doubt, there is no doubt." Remember, each hire represents a significant investment beyond just salary. They reflect your sales culture and will consume resources (onboarding time, pipeline opportunities). Trust your process and keep recruiting to find candidates worth the investment.

Compensation

When making an offer, understand the market rate for the labor you need and the value you'll get from hires. Your compensation structure should align with your sales mechanics and deal sizes.

Variable Compensation

Most sales roles follow a base/commission split:

- 50/50 for new-business acquisition AEs
- 60/40 or 70/30 for SDRs or account managers

Quotas focus reps on revenue-generating activities. While modern CRM tools provide better activity tracking, quotas still serve to incentivize performance.

SDR Compensation

In the San Francisco Bay Area:

- Base: $45k–$55k
- OTE: $65k–$75k

For higher-ticket items, adjust upwards. Compensation is typically based on appointments set and held. Don't cap attainment—if someone can set more appointments, let them.

AE Compensation

For new business acquisition:

- 50/50 split between base and variable
- San Francisco SaaS AE example:
    - Base: $50k–$60k
    - OTE: $100k–$120k

Quota should keep cost of sales under 20% of revenue. For example:

- $100k OTE ($50k variable)
- Required bookings: $500k/year
- Commission rate: 10%
- Monthly quota: $42k

Ensure quotas are attainable. Be prepared to adjust based on actual performance data. Consider Jason Lemkin's approach:

1. Competitive base ($4k/month)
2. No commission until rep covers their cost (125% of base)
3. Then pay 2x commission (20% instead of 10%)
4. 25% commission for cash up front

Pay commissions on cash received, not just bookings.

Equity

While sales roles focus on cash compensation, consider offering some equity to instill an ownership mindset. A few basis points vested over four years is typical, less than engineering or product roles.

Remember, compensation structures may need adjusting as you gather more data. Be flexible and generous with early reps, but maintain a unified plan based on market comps and business economics.

Offering and Closing Candidates

I recommend a two-step process:

1. Verbal offer via phone
2. Formal offer letter once interest is confirmed

For rejections, simply state it "wasn't a fit." Avoid giving detailed reasons to prevent potential legal issues.

When proceeding with an offer, I prefer to:

- State what we pay and the rationale upfront
- Aim for consistency in compensation for similar roles
- Get verbal agreement before sending an offer letter

On negotiation:

- Prefer not to negotiate if the offer is principles-based and fair
- Sell other aspects: personal development, career progression
- Consider offering a role/salary review after six months

After Closing

Move quickly to maintain momentum:

- Minimize time between offer acceptance and start date
- Aim for groups of new hires starting together
- Prepare for successful onboarding:
    1. Line up materials and assign pre-work
    2. Include new hires in team social events

Remember, they're not truly "on the team" until they start working. Treat inbound hires with urgency, just as you would a pending sales deal.

Sales hiring is crucial for your organization's revenue success. Approach it methodically, aiming for high-quality staff who match your go-to-market strategy. Haphazard hiring sabotages your chances of success.

CHAPTER 12

High-Impact Sales Onboarding & Training

After investing time and energy in hiring sales staff, the next step is to maximize your investment by getting new hires up to speed quickly.

WHY ONBOARDING MATTERS

In early-stage B2B sales post product/market fit, your biggest cost is missed or delayed sales. This is especially true in greenfield markets where it's a landgrab. A poorly on-boarded salesperson isn't generating the $50k-$200k a month they could be. Consider the future value of those customers as they recur and refer others, and the lost revenue becomes even more significant.

Losing 30%-50% of each sales class to flameouts, partly due to faulty onboarding, means eating this opportunity cost repeatedly. The lack of rigor around sales onboarding in many organizations is astounding.

Don't rush new hires to face customers; you'll burn good leads and injure their confidence. For experienced hires, don't assume their past expertise is sufficient. You don't know what bad habits they've picked up or what gaps exist in their market knowledge.

Instead, design a rigorous 1-2 week sales boot camp for each hiring class. Cover business and product expertise, presentation skills, objection handling, and CRM proficiency. This investment in proper onboarding will pay off in the long run.

ONBOARDING 101

Run a "university"-style onboarding with cohorts. This creates both competition and camaraderie. Hire in classes and run your onboarding as classes too. Your curriculum should evolve as your go-to-market strategy does, but generally cover these areas:

1. Pre-work
2. Standard Administrative Work
3. Cultural Onboarding
4. Business and Subject-Matter Onboarding
5. Product and Presentation Onboarding

Pre-work

Capitalize on new hires' excitement by assigning pre-work. This can include:

- Watching demo recordings (both good and bad examples)
- Reading relevant materials (blog posts, support documentation)
- Studying assigned books (e.g., "The Goal", "Getting Things Done")

Make it clear that completion will be monitored and tested. Deliver materials in a trackable format, like a shared Google Doc.

Prepare their workspace in advance, complete with necessary tech, materials (notebooks, pens), and company swag. This sets the right tone from day one.

Standard Administrative Work

Handle paperwork (W-2s, payroll setup, stock forms) side-by-side to avoid confusion and delays. I recommend setting aside time for side-by-side execution with each new hire to get this out of the way. Unfamiliar forms can be confusing, which is unpleasant for new hires and risks casting a pall over the rest of your onboarding.

Cultural Onboarding

Explicitly discuss your organization's values. At TalentBin, we emphasized three key tenets:

1. Operating with an engineering mindset: Identify constraints, propose solutions, test them, and embrace or reject the outcome.

2. Being product managers of our sales organization: Prioritize resolving issues based on their impact on revenue.

3. Valuing intellectual honesty: Embrace eyes-wide-open self-assessment, regardless of the outcome.

Frame these values within your organization's history and trajectory. Start articulating these tenets in your hiring process to attract good fits and allow bad fits to self-select out.

Business and Market Subject-Matter Onboarding

Your sales staff needs to be experts in the market, business drivers, and technical realities of your solution to sell authoritatively. Focus on these key areas—market understanding, business driver understanding, and technical understanding.

Market Understanding

Ensure your staff understands:

- The field your solution operates in
- How it has evolved
- Major solution vendors in your space

For example, in human capital management, cover job boards, recruiting workflow software, and HCM cloud suites.

Business Driver Understanding

Train your staff on:

- Key business drivers your solution addresses
- How client businesses work
- Common metrics for measuring these drivers

For instance, in recruiting, metrics might include cost per hire, time to hire, and hiring funnel drop-off.

At TalentBin, we had a former technical recruiter give a comprehensive "Brad Class" on all things recruiting.

Technical Understanding

Familiarize your team with key technological drivers in your space. Focus on the most important terms and innovations to provide a base layer of information.

For TalentBin, this meant ensuring staff could differentiate between front-end and back-end technologies, SQL and NoSQL, etc.

Product and Presentation Onboarding

After establishing the market context, dive into your specific solution:

1. Initial Product Walk-Through: Use an abridged version of your customer-facing demo to correlate product elements with use cases and business drivers.

2. Sales Presentation and Segments: Break down your presentation into chapters, explaining the intention of each and how slides support these goals.

3. Customer-Facing Demo and Demo Segments: Conduct a mock demonstration, contextualizing each section to show how features solve specific business pains.

4. Objection Handling: Rather than covering all possible objections, fold common ones into other sections of onboarding.

5. Competition: If relevant, review the competitive landscape after covering market, business drivers, technology, and product sections.

Remember, the goal is to prepare your staff for compelling, consultative conversations with prospects from the start.

Tools and Process Onboarding

Don't underestimate the importance of training in tools and processes. Modern sales reps should be software-enabled, highly levered professionals. An average day includes office basics like email and calendaring, sales standards like Salesforce.com, and more advanced software like email tracking and presentation tools.

Provisioning & Configuration

Pre-provision all necessary hardware and software before new hires arrive. This includes:

- Desk (sitting or standing), chair or standing foot pad and task stool
- Laptop, external monitor, laptop stand, keyboard, mouse (with navigation buttons)
- Desk phone, headset
- Lab notebook (graph paper preferred), pen cup, high-quality pens
- Software accounts (Google Apps, Salesforce, email tracking like Yesware, presentation software like ClearSlide)
- Schwag (shirts, hoodies, water bottles, coffee mugs, pint glasses, pens, Post-its)

Pre-provisioning sets the tone—you mean business and have a culture of preparation—we are organized, and we don't waste time. The salary expense of quality sales staff far outstrips the capital cost of quality equipment.

Hold a "configuration party" with your new cohort to set up:

- Google Chrome (proper bookmarking, plugins like Rapportive)
- Gmail (signatures, keyboard shortcuts, "undo send," "send and archive," auto-advance)
- Voice mail

- Screenshotting tools (like Jing)
- Corporate email on mobile devices
- Demo environment in the product they'll be selling

Training: Basic Tools

Browser

Train on efficient use of Google Chrome—closing tabs that are no longer needed, creating new windows for new "tasks," closing windows when tasks are complete, and mastering keyboard shortcuts.

Email for Sales

Teach "Getting Things Done" for email management. Cover:

- Writing clear emails (topical subject lines, proper CC usage, formatting for readability)
- Templating for efficiency (create a culture of template sharing)
- Gmail keyboard shortcuts (J/K to navigate, X to select, E to archive, C to compose, etc.)
- Proofreading and grammatical excellence in client-facing communication

Calendaring for Sales

Train on:

- Sending meeting invites with clear information (venue, actionable title, agenda items)
- Calendar hygiene (removing irrelevant items, blocking prep and follow-up time)
- "Painting the calendar" to manage time effectively and ensure focus on important tasks

Training: Sales-Specific Tools

CRM (e.g., Salesforce)

Establish the rule: "If it's not in Salesforce, it doesn't count." Cover:

- Data model: accounts, contacts, opportunities, leads, activities
- Creating objects and important fields (projected revenue, stage, contact information)
- Key reports and task views (pipeline reports, error-checking reports)
- Proper dispositioning of items (marking demo events as "held," retiring tasks, noting closed won/lost opportunities)

Sales-Enabled Email

Demonstrate:

- BCC'ing to CRM for record keeping
- Templating and mass mailing for efficiency
- Open and click tracking for deal insights
- How email activity is recorded and reported to track rep activity levels

Presentation Software

Cover common use cases:

- Sending meeting credentials via calendar invite or email
- Using and modifying standard slide decks
- Executing live screenshares
- Recording pitches for later audit or to send to absent contacts
- Post-presentation follow-up (sending instrumented deck hyperlinks, dispositioning demo notes)

Power Dialing Software

If applicable, cover use cases for market development reps (quickly cycling through prospect lists, leaving pre-recorded voicemails, sending follow-up emails) and account executives (reaching contacts directly from Salesforce, dispositioning tasks and notes).

Remember, you won't cover every scenario in training. The goal is to ensure reps understand each tool's purpose, where it fits in their process, and its key workflows. Continuous learning through doing is essential.

Sales Cycle and Cadence

It's crucial that new reps understand how and when to use tools in the sales cycle. Cover your organization's specific process and cadence:

- Typical time to close a deal
- Bottoms-up or tops-down approach
- Responsibilities in the sales cycle
- Number of presentations required
- Use of trials or pilots
- When to close an unproductive opportunity

Review your team's weekly, monthly, and quarterly rhythm, including meetings and their goals.

DRILLING, REPETITIONS, & SHADOWING

Practice is crucial. Implement:

1. Group Drilling: Have each rep present each chapter of the presentation/demo, with feedback from you and the team.
2. Sparring: Pair reps to practice as presenter and prospect, using actual tools they'll use with real prospects.
3. Pair Programming/Ride-Alongs: Pair new hires with seasoned reps to follow key workflows in a "production" environment.

Bluebirding, Ramp, and Monitoring

As new reps go live:

1. Assign "bluebird" opportunities with high closing likelihood.
2. Team with reps on early calls for backup.
3. Use unqualified leads as practice demos.
4. Implement proactive and ambient call review using recording tools.
5. Track KPIs and conduct regular one-on-ones.

Ongoing Learning & Development

Continue investing in learning after onboarding:

1. Schedule regular coaching sessions (e.g., an hour on Friday afternoons).
2. Focus on professional development, especially for SDRs who might become AEs.
3. Keep reps updated on product releases and market changes.
4. Embed updates into regular meetings or schedule special training events.

Remember, the biggest cost to a young sales organization that has hit product/market fit is the opportunity cost of missed or delayed sales. Rigorous, thoughtful onboarding and ongoing development will minimize these costs, speed up time to revenue for new reps, increase retention, and enhance team cohesion and excellence.

CHAPTER 13

Where Do You Go From Here?

Congratulations! If you're successfully scaling up your sales operation, you have moved beyond this book's scope. You're now a bona-fide sales professional, and if you have sellers successfully closing business under you, you're a "Sales Leader."

Am I Ready to Hire a Sales Manager?

Before professionalizing your sales organization, ensure you've met the exit criteria:

- You have sellers successfully selling your solution at least as well as you were.
- You've proven "repeatability" with one to three sellers.

This repeatability is powerful—it shows investors you can turn their money into revenue-generating salespeople. If you haven't proven this yet, you're not ready for professional sales management. As the person who cracked the sales code, you're best positioned to teach others.

Who Should I Hire?

When ready, look for a "tactical sales leader":

- Someone currently running a single sales team (e.g., 6 AEs) or a director overseeing multiple teams.

- From a scaled startup in your space or a tangential one, with similar sales motion and Average Selling Price.
- Avoid hiring from large, established companies.

This is a critical hire—reference check thoroughly. Once onboard, your job is to help them ingest your documented sales process and quickly manage the team successfully. You're now the Manager of the Sales Manager.

FURTHER READING

Founding Sales was written because there wasn't yet a tactical textbook for early stage sales, written specifically for founders and other non-sellers. But there's a whole constellation of high quality sales books for sales professionals, of which my favorites are listed below. I highly recommend you check them out to help further your sales education.

1. Selling:
    - The Transparency Sale (Caponi)
    - The Challenger Sale (Dixon & Adamson)
    - Triangle Selling (Bray & Sorey)
    - SPIN Selling (Rackham)

2. Sales Management:
    - Cracking the Sales Management Code (Jordan)
    - The Revenue Acceleration Formula (Roberge)
    - Blueprints For A SaaS Sales Organization (VanderKooij)

3. Prospecting & SDR Management:
    - The Sales Development Playbook (Bertuzzi)
    - Leading Sales Development (Donovan & Homison)
    - Fanatical Prospecting (Blount)

4. Startup Sales:
    - David Skok's writing on his blog *forEntrepreneurs.com* is also quite good when it comes to a very clear, tactical early stage go-to-market education.

www.ingramcontent.com/pod-product-compliance
Lightning Source LLC
Chambersburg PA
CBHW050225100526
44585CB00017BA/2014